THE
WORSHIP
REVOLUTION

KEITH DUNCAN

ISBN: 0-9786581-8-3
978-09786581-8-2

Published by

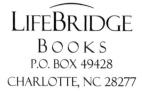

LIFEBRIDGE
BOOKS
P.O. BOX 49428
CHARLOTTE, NC 28277

Printed in the United States of America.

DEDICATION

This book is dedicated to the lasting memory of Dr. David Horton—a Kingdom Psalmist—who represented this new breed of Worship Revolutionaries God is raising up. I thank you for taking the time to impart into my life the many lessons you had come to embrace in your own ministry. May the seeds you have sown into countless men and women yield a perpetual harvest that will be credited to your account.

To the many worshipers who are in the midst of this season of change—those who have been crying out in the night hour for more of God's presence—may this book only fuel the fire God has placed within you. I pray that you will pay the price and accept the challenge to join the Worship Revolution.

To my son, Judah, your name means *praise.* You are my prophetic psalmist in training. I pray you will discover your purpose at a young age and begin to walk in the plans to which God calls you. May you see the heavens opened as you sow the seed of praise into all the regions of the world. I love you, son, and am so very proud of you.

Last but certainly not least, I dedicate this book to the love of my life, and woman of my dreams. Michele, I thank you for the countless hours you have laughed and

3

cried with me. Our journey has definitely been one of adventure. In the good times and the bad, you stood faithfully by my side proving to be the perfect helpmate. I am thankful for your continual love, and I look forward to sharing the rest of our journey to the Throne Room together. I love you forever.

— *Keith Duncan*

A NOTE FROM MYLES MONROE
— MY SPIRITUAL FATHER AND MENTOR

The need to redefine true worship
from a Kingdom perspective and give
meaning once again to what it means to enter
the courts of a king in our 21st Century humanistic
world is imperative. Keith has effectively responded to
the challenge in this classic work and his combination
of personal, practical, and theological approach to this
subject makes an engaging experience for the reader.
This book is a must for the serious worshiper.

– *Dr. Myles Munroe*
Nassau, Bahamas

CONTENTS

Chapter One

The Journey to a Vision

Obviously, the church I was raised in was desperate for a musician! If not, why would they ask me—an eleven year old boy—to play the piano?

Actually, I started on keyboards when I was six—the same age I gave my heart to the Lord and asked Him to be my personal Savior.

I was an unprofessional musician by today's standards, yet people were kind and constantly encouraged my gift. From this small beginning, God began to stir within me the purpose of who I am and what He called me to be.

Being a worship leader was not a career I dreamed of having—it just grew and developed within me and became part of my spiritual DNA.

DISCOVERING GOD'S PURPOSE

I was raised in a traditional denominational church where people didn't stray far from the hymn book. As a teen I loved Southern Gospel music and began to play with quartets. We soon formed a band and did some traveling.

The Lord in His wisdom used this as a foundational block and an important stepping stone to develop my ear for harmony, cadences, chord progressions, improvising and components of music He would later use for His glory.

Young and single, my friends and I would be at the church until nearly midnight on Saturday nights, working on special music for the Sunday morning service. It gave me an outlet I enjoyed, a place to belong and allowed me to discover my purpose on this earth.

Myles Munroe, my spiritual father, wisely says, "The worst thing in life is not death; rather, it is going through life without knowing your purpose."

I totally concur. Without this clear knowledge, our existence becomes merely an experiment.

The Lord graciously called me to become a minister of music and I began to serve Him in churches across the nation.

TOTALLY UNEXPECTED

It was May, 1997.

I was now married to my beautiful wife and partner in ministry, Michele. She and I had been serving a congregation in Newport News, Virginia, for approximately six months. Up to this point my strength had been developing choirs and performing choral music. I didn't really understand what it meant to "flow" in worship.

Things were about to change!

During a service one particular Sunday night, the power and presence of the Lord enveloped the room in a manner which was totally unexpected.

I really don't know how to describe it other than there was a holy, awesome entrance of God's power which filled the sanctuary.

I was standing at the keyboard and began to play the sounds I was hearing from above. The next thing I knew, I found myself face down on the floor.

What happened to me that night transformed my life and charted my future in ways I never expected.

THE VISION

As I lay prostrate on the floor, God allowed me to see a vision I will never forget. The church service continued, but for me, the sanctuary was converted into the Throne Room of God.

I saw the gleaming marble floors and the stairs leading up to the heavenly throne itself—and the legs of the One Who was seated there. I knew immediately I was in the presence of God.

While I was transported to this awesome place, over in the back right hand corner of our church, someone began to sing. It was a woman with a tiny, thin "church mouse" voice who began to offer her unrehearsed, spontaneous song to the Lord. And as the sound sprang forth, I noticed on the Throne Room floor what I can only describe as a brilliant diamond-shaped object that would just spin like a top. Yet, when her voice silenced, the diamond disappeared.

Then, as she began to sing again, a powerful wave of God's glory swept across the sanctuary, and those sparkling diamonds reappeared on the floor of the Throne Room.

WITH ONE VOICE!

While the Lord was giving me this revelation, the people in our church began singing with one voice. It was the sound of many voices singing their own unique and individual praise, and yet, it sounded as one singular voice. This was the most melodious music I had ever heard.

The power of the worship seemed to ebb and flow as the congregation presented their song to the Lord.

With each wave, more of the diamonds in my vision appeared on the floor, eventually covering the entire Throne Room of God. When the crescendo of worship increased, I noticed these sparkling diamonds began to move—as if they were dancing! Next, I saw a substance resembling milk and honey flowing from the One Who sat upon the throne. It poured onto the floor among the diamonds, yet never once did it disturb these sparkling gems.

The service lasted for nearly two hours—and it was the beginning of a personal transformation in my life and music ministry.

REFLECTORS OF HIS LIGHT

What I experienced that memorable night was so incredible, I hesitated to speak of it publicly, but shared it with my wife and the pastor.

From that moment forward, the Lord began to open my heart and flood my soul with the true meaning of heavenly worship. He even began to reveal Hebrew words I had never before known. One term in particular is *halal*—which means "to shine, to make a boast, to be clamorously foolish." The literal translation is "to spin like a top," which is exactly what the diamonds were doing in my vision.

Now, when believers begin to worship the Lord, I see them as reflectors of light before the throne—mirroring the brilliance of the Source.

As we move into His courts, we shine and even boast of the glory of the Lord, radiating the majesty of the King.

God also continues to remind me, "Movement from My throne does not take place until the people release their worship. The church has been praying for My river to flow, but they have held back the one thing I am looking for—worship."

"WE ARE GOING AFTER GOD!"

The pastor of the church we were serving also caught the vision and was open to what the Lord desired for this body of Christ.

He had birthed the church and served as the senior minster for many years, but on a Sunday morning he stood before the people and announced, "I must confess. I've been more concerned over what you, the congregation, think about the service than God's opinion." Then he added, "I'm making a choice and a decision today. We are going after God."

The Lord honors authority, and because the pastor blessed what God was revealing to me, we were able to make the dynamic shift from a choir-oriented music program to a true worship experience.

The vision I was allowed to see rocked my world and changed everything I'd been taught concerning church music. It was as if I was having an identity crisis, yet the Lord knew exactly what He was doing.

When I came on board, the choir had approximately 30 members. However, because of programs, we experienced explosive growth to the point we were traveling to other churches and camp meetings with the choir, praise dancers, the banner ministry and a full band. We had to organize tour buses to accommodate over 100 people who were involved in our music efforts.

There was much excitement and people were coming out of the woodwork to be part of what was taking place.

Purge the Choir?

Then came the visitation from heaven, where instead of the choir and a dazzling production being the highlight, the focus was on the King.

———— ♔ ————

I remember the day the Lord asked, "Keith, are you willing to let Me purge the choir?"

"Of course, Lord," I responded—thinking perhaps four or five would not be able to make the transition from a performance-oriented choir to where God was leading in worship.

It wasn't just five, ten or fifteen members whom the Lord purged. Before long the number was pared down to a small, but dedicated troupe. They understood their Levitical role to offer their praise and lead the people to the throne of God.

"His Call"

The vision I received at this Spirit-directed church in Virginia became a major turning-point and allowed the Lord to direct my wife and I into *His Call*, the international ministry we are privileged to enjoy today as worship missionaries.

As a result, thousands of church leaders and musicians are experiencing this same transformation at our conferences and events in the United States and the nations of the world. They are becoming keepers of the flame.

Looking back, we can see God's hand at work every step of the way. In fact, six years before my vision, while serving a large church in North Carolina, a woman in the congregation who was a prayer warrior placed a card on my desk which read, "Forever Answering His Call."

Those words, "His Call," leapt into my spirit—because my passion was to follow the Lord wherever He was leading. Immediately, I had those two words personalized on my licence plate as a constant reminder I was following Him.

CHEERING FOR THE LORD!

During this same year, on a Friday evening, I went with our youth group to a baseball game at the Charlotte Knight's stadium.

While there, I became rather bored—looking around at the people and watching the mascot instead of the game. Then, all of a sudden, the ball field seemed to change before my eyes. Between first and third base, I saw a platform set up as if it was being prepared for a Billy Graham crusade.

This was a scene the Lord was allowing me to visualize. The stadium was bursting to capacity and the people were cheering—not for the athletes, but for the Almighty!

Even before God gave me the revelation of what true worship entails, that night I saw stadiums packed with people who were passionate to come into the Lord's presence.

I believe God was arresting my attention, giving me food for thought to prepare my heart and mind for the momentous days ahead.

THE ATMOSPHERE OF HEAVEN

What you are about to read is not a "how to" book to become a better minister of music or a more informed member of the congregation as you participate in praise and worship.

I am praying you will open your heart and allow the Lord to give you a passion for His reality beyond anything you have ever known.

If you are tired of the status quo and weary of going through the motions, the Lord is ready to lift you into the very atmosphere of heaven—not just when you are in corporate worship, but in your daily walk with Him.

Are you ready for this exciting journey?

CHAPTER TWO

A PASSION FOR HIS PRESENCE

This is a momentous time in the history of the church. An exciting spiritual shift is awakening the body of Christ. Believers are rising up because they are hungry and passionate for the presence of God.

We have referred to this group in the past as being a *remnant*; those who are thirsting and seeking after the things of God and the face of the Almighty—zealous for His purposes, pursuing His agenda and plans. This once was a small minority and only the few, the *brave*, ever dared to take this remnant deeper.

YOUR ENTRANCE

For decades, the pattern has been for churches to

17

present a polished program which appeals to the masses so the membership can grow and we can build bigger ministries in the name of evangelism. However, if the truth were told, we are just transitioning people from one church to the next, never taking them any further in faith or in their relationship with the Lord.

The concept and purpose of what the "worship revolution" is about deals particularly with going deep into the very presence of God. It's primary focus is not necessarily evangelical in nature, although evangelism does occur as a result.

The bottom line for many churches—and the jugular vein of their reason for being—is seeing people come to know Christ, yet life does not end and the Kingdom does not stop at the entrance to the heavenlies. It's merely an important starting point.

What we will discuss on these pages is to take those who have become born again into the Throne Room of God.

"ADVANCE THE KINGDOM!"

The *remnant* of the church has been in hiding far too long—as if they have been secluded in a spiritual cave.

They've been silenced for a season, but now God is causing them to venture out of the caverns and is allowing their silence to be broken with a shout of praise and a voice of victory. Their battle cry is simply this: "Advance the Kingdom!"

This worship revolution is designed to take those who have confessed Christ as their personal Savior into a far more intimate relationship with Him. Praise God, the remnant is fast becoming a larger portion of the body and prophetically, I believe eventually they will become the majority.

When this takes place, church as we know it, through its religious structures, dictates and traditions, will come to a close—or it will be greatly challenged. Why? Because people within this growing remnant will no longer be satisfied with their "forms" of worship. They're hungry for only one thing—time with their King and passionate for the presence of God.

APPEALING TO THE MASSES?

Having served in churches as a full time minister of music for nearly two decades, I have worked with several pastors and understand the necessity of the *functions* of the church and all this entails: baby dedications, weddings, funerals, fund raising, publications. But where is there time to bask in the fullness of the Almighty? How do we allow the people an opportunity to drink from the fountain of the Spirit—those who are thirsting for more?

When do we give them a chance to *practice* entering into the Throne Room of heaven?

In far too many of our churches, we have used and adopted the pattern of man and commercialization for the purposes of appealing to the masses.

We've taken the forms and practices which seem to have been productive and have made them our standard. Consequently, we go to one church and they're singing all of Israel Houghton's music. Or they're using only Darlene Zschech's songs, or those of Paul Baloche. People who are involved in worship music today will recognize these names.

The writing of these dedicated individuals is a definite contribution to the body of Christ, but if we are not careful, the purpose will no longer be the message, rather what is singable and recognizable. This is because we have entered into a "seeker sensitive" era and want people to feel comfortable—able to sing the songs without having to project the lyrics up on the screens or print them in our bulletins.

However, there is much more to worship.

THE HEAVENLY PATTERN

If we look at Revelation 4 and 5, we begin to better understand there is a pattern which has been established —in which the very manifest presence of God resides.

John the Revelator gives us these descriptions as he begins to pen the lyrics and sounds of heaven. Attempting to translate a spiritual concept into a physical realm is quite a task, yet John heard the words of the songs echoing from above.

Christ is the centrality of his worship and the message of heaven is geared toward His attributes, His holiness and His righteousness.

- *"Holy, holy, holy, Lord God Almighty, Who was and is and is to come"* (Revelation 4:8).
- *"You are worthy, O Lord, to receive glory and honor and power"* (v.11).
- *"Behold, the Lion of the tribe of Judah"* (Revelation 5:5).

- *"Worthy is the Lamb who was slain..."* (v.12).
- He is the *"Alpha and the Omega, the Beginning and the End"* (Revelation 21:6).

John was allowed to see the place where God rests—where worship continues 24/7 – 365 days a year! As we will discuss in the next chapter, it gives us an intimate glimpse of the heavenly pattern of worship.

WHAT ABOUT GOD'S OPINION?

My question and challenge is, why are so many worship leaders today expecting to find the presence of God but never following the pattern?

When we adopt man's blueprint, the end result is nothing more than human ability. As a result, we focus our worship songs and the very heartbeat upon man and what we desire. "I'm gonna get my blessing," and "This is what I need," and, "Gimme this—Gimme that."

Is it any wonder why we have so many worship leaders, congregations and church officials suffering such moral failure? When we sow to the flesh we reap corruption.

Of course, there are still excellent "role model" churches doing amazing things in the Kingdom.

However, we must understand the body of Christ has many functions; just as an arm, a leg and an eye each has a specific purpose.

The problem is that we often relegate worship to the mass level of the opinion of man which results in the secularization of Christianity. Soon we squeeze the manifest, tangible presence of God completely out of our worship experiences because we want people to feel warm and fuzzy in the sanctuary. Often we are more sensitive to man's opinion than we are God's view of our services. Consequently, we receive only human results!

It's All About Him!

Thankfully, we are now entering a period of divine transition. We are nearing the point on the prophetic timeline of God's plan when the church is gearing for a major paradigm shift.

No longer are we going to look to man to set the agenda, but there is a remnant waiting to understand and discover the pattern of worship as it is in the heavens.

Many have decided they are going to pay the price and adopt this model of worship from above. They will create a "resting place" for His presence on earth. They will be pursuing God with lyrics which focus primarily and exclusively upon Him, His worthiness, His holiness, His righteousness.

"WE BLESS YOUR NAME"

God loves to hear His praises and as we begin to build this place of worship on earth—in our sanctuaries, homes, automobiles and offices—we will discover the fullness of His power, His glory and the strength of His might.

Why is this true? Because the Lord has entered our house. No longer will we have to worry over motivating people into a frenzy of emotion. Yes, worship touches our feelings, but it's not whipped-up *emotionalism.*

Instead, here is what we must declare as a body of believers:

"Oh, you are holy, O sovereign God. Worthy in Your righteousness, holy in Your power, sovereign in Your might. Oh, we declare You as King of kings and Lord of lords and forever You shall reign upon the earth and in the heavens. Oh, when no one was worthy to take the scroll and

open its seven seals, yea, You were there. You, the lion of the tribe of Judah. Oh, we bless Your Name, Lord."

AROUND THE SON!

Now is the time for a revolution!

The dictionary has several definitions of this word, some of which relate to uprising and upheaval. A revolution also applies to our solar system—how the earth and the planets orbit the sun.

The worship revolution, however, orbits around the Son. It is also a *holy* uprising of those who are starved for the presence of God, who are no longer made satisfied and complete by sitting near the streams of relaxation and comfort. They have an inner passion and a burning desire for their worship to be totally centered upon Him.

The adoration and praise they release will truly revolve around the Son of God and it will declare His majesty and glory.

CHAPTER THREE

ON EARTH AS IT IS IN HEAVEN

T hrough the years, I've seen many ministers of music using pop culture to determine and dictate what their program is going to resemble. In effect, they're announcing, "We need to be relevant and cutting edge, so we want you to sing this artist's music. He (or she) has a fresh, contemporary sound and that's what people today are looking for."

Unfortunately, when we allow a "seeker sensitive" paradigm to go too far, we may create an atmosphere where people feel comfortable, yet we totally miss the mark of what true worship is all about.

Worship is not singing the most current, popular hip hop, "phat," over-the-top-tunes. Instead, it must be all about our Heavenly Father—and what *He* desires.

The danger of allowing our culture to dictate our presentation, is that we can become very egocentric in our focus. When this happens, everything we do in our worship experience glorifies the ego, man—dealing and speaking only to the person and his or her needs.

Don't get me wrong. There is a time for personal ministry in our local church, but I believe the Lord wants to challenge us to enter a new dimension; to steer away from *us* and enter into *Him*.

I am convinced worship is our ministry to the Lord. It should never be about us.

THE MISSING COMPONENT

Hopefully, you can distinguish the difference between worship and preaching.

The *preached* Word is to strengthen, develop and disciple us as believers. It centers on our needs and how we can move into practicing a lifestyle of holiness and righteousness, overcoming obstacles.

Worship, however, is centered on the King.

If this is our understanding and it is true, why do we spend so little time in praise and worship and much more on the preached Word?

Without question, I believe with all my heart the Word of God is essential to our daily lives, however, there is a missing component churches are failing to connect with. Instead of an egocentric theme which predominates our worship experiences every Sunday, we should seek to make our worship *theocentric*. It must evolve and take "revolutions" around the majesty of our King, the great Jehovah. Everything we release as worship should be directed toward Almighty God as opposed to our "feel good" inclinations.

WHERE ARE YOU LEADING?

In understanding worship, I recognize you have to meet people where they are as a worship leader and relate one on one—leading them where they need to be. However, we have too many ministers of music who, although sincere, have no idea what the true objective is. As a result, the *remnant* is no longer satisfied with going through the motions and with dancing around the outer courts of praise.

The grassroots worship movement the Lord is raising up, is pleading, "Give us the presence of God lest we die."

It's a revolutionary cry: "We want worship, not a

circus. Don't offer us a religious 'form' or a theological display. We want the anointed, tangible and manifested presence of God rather than the fallible practice of man."

This is why it is so imperative we raise up worship leaders who know *where* to lead the congregation using a meaningful worship experience. Where is that place? Let me remind you it is a revolution which revolves around the Son, our great God. Hallelujah!

No More "Score Cards"

Sometimes we even allow our *religious* background to dictate what worship is all about. I thank God for writers whom God is using to pen songs and release them to the body of Christ. But we should be careful not to worship the artists, nor what they have created. Instead, we must allow chosen, gifted people to help cultivate and develop the heart of worship. If this is our earnest cry it will forever change the way we approach the throne of God.

No longer should we be attending church to get a spiritual "high" or enter with our score cards to rate the worship service.

It's not about our personal preferences, nor does it matter whether they sing our favorite song at the exact tempo we enjoy. "Well, I really wasn't moved today because it didn't give me goose bumps."

Let me remind you once again, the spotlight of worship should never shine on you and me; it is always directed toward the Almighty. That's why we must prayerfully discern and hear with spiritual ears rather than spending our time pondering what we think of the service.

In the final analysis, God is the Chief Judge of our offerings of praise and adoration. Since this is a performance for the King, let's honor and present His Majesty with what He deserves and expects.

"COME UP HERE"

Look closely at what John saw in his revelation. *"I looked, and behold, a door standing open in heaven. And the first voice which I heard was like a trumpet speaking with me, saying, "Come up here, and I will show you things which must take place..."* (Revelation 4:1).

Then John begins to describe in detail what it looks like in heaven: *"Around the throne were twenty-four thrones, and on the thrones I saw twenty-four elders sitting, clothed in white robes; and they had crowns of gold on their heads. And from the throne proceeded lightnings, thunderings, and voices. Seven lamps of fire were burning before the throne, which are the seven Spirits of God. Before the throne there was a sea of glass, like crystal"* (vv.4-6).

John also reveals, *"The four living creatures, each having six wings, were full of eyes around and within. And they do not rest day or night, saying: 'Holy, holy, holy, Lord God Almighty, Who was and is and is to come!' Whenever the living creatures give glory and honor and thanks to Him who sits on the throne, who lives forever and ever, the twenty-four elders fall down before Him who sits on the throne and worship Him who lives forever and ever, and cast their crowns before the throne, saying: "You are worthy, O Lord, to receive glory and honor and power; For You created all things, and by Your will they exist and were created"* (vv.8-11).

STOPPED AT THE ENTRANCE

This revelation gives us the *posture* of worship. The Greek word for worship is *proskuneo,* which literally means to kiss the hand—as a dog kisses the hand of his master.

This typifies the affection and adoration which needs to be prevalent in our worship today, but where is it? Why do we rarely seem to capture the very essence of what God is seeking?

Most churches do not set aside enough time to truly lead people into the presence of the Lord. I've had many worship ministers ask me, "How can I move people to the Throne Room when our pastor allows just fifteen minutes for congregational worship and a song by the choir—then it's time for the offering?"

Sadly, we don't give ample opportunity to drink freely at the wells of worship.

We sing and dance around the outer courts of celebration and praise—just going in circles. Then, when we finally reach the very entrance to the Throne Room, we have to stop to "change the order of the service" because we have used our allotted minutes.

MORE THAN A MESSAGE

Some worship leaders are guilty too—taking people just so far, then quenching the Spirit. Why? Because they do not understand, or perhaps have never personally experienced, where God wants His people to be.

To add to the problem, many pastors think people come only to hear the message—and this is what the members have been taught. Of course we need to embrace the Word, yet God is looking for the time when He can receive the worship due Him.

*I pray, as we delve into what
the Lord has to say pertaining to praise
and worship, you will receive the direction
and guidance necessary to usher your
congregation into God's holy presence.*

For all who are participants in worship, let me encourage you to open your heart and experience here on earth the glory which is continually taking place in heaven.

CHAPTER FOUR

IN SPIRIT AND
IN TRUTH

There is a brief story in the New Testament that contains a particularly powerful message—and a parallel of life or death for the church today.

Allow me to share what the Spirit revealed to me from the Word.

After Jesus' triumphal entry into Jerusalem where the people followed Him shouting, *"Hosanna! Blessed is He who comes in the name of the Lord"* (Mark 11:9), He journeyed with His disciples to spend the night in Bethany.

The next morning, as they were walking back to Jerusalem, Jesus was hungry, and from a distance He saw a fig tree with leaves on its branches. But as He drew closer it became apparent there was no fruit, only leaves,

"...for it was not the season for figs" (v.13).

In response, Jesus spoke to the tree, saying, *"Let no one eat fruit from you ever again"* (v.14)—and the disciples heard His words.

One day later, they passed by the exact same spot and *"...saw the fig tree dried up from the roots"* (v.20).

Peter, remembering what Jesus had earlier spoken, exclaimed, *"Rabbi, Look! The fig tree which You cursed has withered away"* (v.21).

MOVING MOUNTAINS

This was the perfect opportunity for Jesus to teach a lesson to His disciples. He answered, *"Have faith in God. For assuredly, I say to you, whoever says to this mountain, 'Be removed and be cast into the sea,' and does not doubt in his heart, but believes that those things he says will be done, he will have whatever he says. Therefore I say to you, whatever things you ask when you pray, believe that you receive them, and you will have them"* (vv.22-24).

For years I have heard these verses used when teaching on the topic of faith, but one day as I was reading it in context —including the story of the fig tree—I began to grasp the larger picture.

I had questions. Why would Jesus look for figs from this particular tree when Scripture specifically states it was not the harvest season for figs? Wouldn't Jesus—who not only grew up in the society and culture but was the Creator of the world—know this fact?

If so, why did He approach the tree?

WHERE IS OUR FRUIT?

The second thing which came to my mind was, if Jesus, the Omniscient One, knew the fig tree was able to produce fruit, why did He curse the tree? The Lord began to show me He is not limited or controlled by the seasons—so whether we are in the summer or winter of our lives, He wants us to be productive and bear fruit.

As I delved further into the story, the words, *"Jesus was hungry"* (v.12), seemed to pop off the page.

The Son of God was in search of something which would satisfy the hunger pangs so He would have strength to continue on His journey.

The reason Jesus veered from His original route and walked toward the tree (v.13) is because He saw signs of life which told Him it was alive.

Glory to God! When we can't get to the Lord, He will

always find a way to reach us.

*When it seems we are stranded in
the cold winter season, God has a way
of changing His path to find us.*

"Hot Now!"

Jesus faced disappointment. The signs of life on the tree were the bark, the root system and the leaves—yet this is not what He hungered for. His taste buds longed for figs, and nothing else would curb His appetite.

When I'm driving down the road and spy the "Hot Donuts Now," sign illuminated in the window of a Krispy Kreme store, I've been known to make a sharp U-turn and rush right in!

It's not the green lettering on the logo I'm attracted to, but the tasty products waiting on the inside.

If I have a hankering for a donut and the light is off, I am frustrated since I don't want cold donuts which have been sitting on the shelf. I'm salivating for those fresh ones which literally melt in your mouth!

Hungry for Worship

The Lord reminded me of this key Scripture: *"But the*

hour is coming and now is, when the true worshipers will worship the Father in spirit and in truth: for the Father is seeking such to worship Him" (John 4:23).

In the book of Mark, the Son of God was hungry for food, yet in this verse He is hungry for worship —actively seeking those who will come before Him in *spirit*, and in *truth!*

DIVINE GUIDELINES

I've visited churches which demonstrate plenty of spirit and exuberance in their praise. There is celebration and rejoicing, but the *truth* of worship is missing.

This is why we must pursue answers to help us develop genuine worship.

We simply cannot remain complacent and allow our culture to dictate how we approach God's holy presence.

What are these truths? Where do we find divine guidelines? What are some of the parameters for worship?

Recorded in Scripture are several Hebrew words for praise in the Old Testament. Perhaps you are thinking,

While this is true, we find much of the historical writing regarding what took place in the Old Testament became part of the culture in New Testament times. Consequently, it was not discussed because it was a *given*.

There was no need to mention some of these Hebrew principles because they were already taking place in New Testament worship.

SHOUTING AND KNEELING

Let's look at a few of the Hebrew references.

The psalmist writes, *"One generation shall praise Your works to another, and shall declare Your mighty acts"* (Psalm 145:4).

The word for praise is *shabach*, which translated means "address in a loud tone, to command, to triumph, to glory." It literally means *shout!*

We also read, *"Oh come, let us worship and bow down; Let us kneel before the Lord our Maker"* (Psalm 95:6).

"Kneel" in Hebrew is *barak*—to bless God as an act of adoration by physically kneeling before Him. When used in Scripture, it implies expecting to receive a blessing from the Lord, yet it is paying our homage to Him.

How many times have you seen <u>shabach</u> or <u>barak</u> alive and well in your local church services?

Have you witnessed people shouting unto the Lord with the voice of triumph? Or, when was the last occasion, your congregation, overcome with awe, knelt down in holy reverence to bless God?

RAISE YOUR HANDS!

In Psalms we also read, *"Thus I will bless You while I live; I will lift up my hands in Your name"* (Psalm 63:4). The Hebrew for "lift up my hands" is *yadah.* It's a verb with a root meaning, "to throw out; therefore to worship with extended hand."

Does your congregation raise their hands in worship and praise to the Lord?

We lift our arms and show our open, empty hands as a sign of surrender. It's a picture of what we see when an army has captured the enemy.

Are we totally surrendered in our worship services to

41

the King of kings? Are we unashamed and willing to lift up our hands in the sanctuary or bow on bended knee in esteem and honor to our Mighty God?

"CHARGE IT!"

The Bible instructs us, *"Offer to God thanksgiving, and pay your vows to the Most High"* (Psalm 50:14). The thanksgiving or "praise" in this verse is translated from the Hebrew term *towdah*—from the same root word as *yadah,* but more specifically it means "an extension of the hands in adoration, avowal or acceptance."

For application to our lives, it is apparent in the Psalms and elsewhere, *towdah* is used to thank God for things not yet received as well as for what is already at hand.

Are you joyfully lifting your hands to Jehovah, thanking Him in advance for the prophetic promises He has placed within your spirit—even though you have not yet seen the tangible results?

I like what one preacher said: "Praise God on credit because He's good for it!"

When you don't feel you have sufficient praise in your spiritual bank account or have reason for a shout of joy, just say, "Charge it!"

A SPONTANEOUS RELEASE

What the Lord has done for us is definitely worth getting excited over! *"Oh, clap your hands, all you people"* (Psalm 47:1).

"Taqa" is the original term for "clap"—"to strike your hands together, making a loud sound."

In some churches, the only time believers clap is to applaud or commend a performance. Think for a moment and try to recall the last service where the entire congregation clapped their hands in a jubilant shout of praise unto God which was not promoted by a minister or a worship leader who encouraged, "Come on. Let's give the Lord a praise offering!"

What a dramatic difference when our expression to the Almighty overflows from a spontaneous, extemporaneous release of our spirit.

REJOICE! CELEBRATE!

The reason I am sharing these words from the original language is so we will have a fuller understanding of why and how the Lord expects us to enter into His courts with praise and worship.

The psalmist writes, *"Praise the Lord! Praise, O servants of the Lord, praise the name of the Lord!"* (Psalm 113:1).

In this verse, the Hebrew word for praise is *halal*— "To be clear, to shine, to boast, to show, to rave, to celebrate, to make a boast, to be clamorously foolish."

This term is used more than any other in the Old Testament. The literal translation includes, "To spin like a top."

This is what the Lord showed me in my vision —allowing me to see those who worship as brilliant diamonds reflecting God's glory.

Is *halal* expressed in our worship services? Do we see people rejoicing and celebrating, not because some "groove" is being played by the worship team, but because of our heartfelt joy in the Lord?

DAVID DANCED!

When David brought back the Ark of the Covenant after it had been stolen by the Philistines, the presence of God returned to the camp of the Israelites. As a result, he danced before the Lord.

Scripture records, *"...as the ark of the Lord came into the city of David, Michal, Saul's daughter looked through a window, and saw king David leaping and dancing before the Lord"* (2 Samuel 6:16 KJV).

Here, the Hebrew word for dancing is *karar*—"whirling" before Jehovah.

David was so happy to have the presence of God returned, he was expressing *halal* and *karar* at the same time!

If I had been there, I'd be rejoicing, shouting, dancing and praising God with him!

THE POWER OF MUSIC

Being an instrumental player on the keyboard, the Lord uses me in *zamar*—Hebrew for "to touch the strings." We find the word used in many Scriptures, including, *"Be exalted, O Lord, in Your own strength! We will sing and praise* [zamar] *Your power"* (Psalm 21:13).

Not only does this mean to vocally sing, but also to praise God with musical instruments.

There are occasions in the worship experience when I may stop leading the people in song because I feel they are not ready to enter God's presence. At such moments, the Lord directs me to simply play music unto Him.

Remember, David was a harpist and his music would

soothe the soul of King Saul.

I was quite young when I first discovered the role of instrumental music. However, later, when I felt led to play the keyboard with no one singing, some would question, saying, "Keith, all you want to do is show off your piano skills. You're just looking to be in the limelight!"

Through the years the Lord has graciously proven to me again and again the effectiveness and power of instrumental music in worship.

LIFT YOUR VOICE

If you read the last chapter of Psalms, you'll find recorded, *"Let everything that has breath praise the Lord"* (Psalm 150:6).

Perhaps the greatest dimension the Father is looking for in our praise to Him simply comes from our vocal cords and lips.

He wants us to sing unto Him. *"Rejoice in the Lord, O you righteous! For praise from the upright is beautiful"* (Psalm 33:1).

In this passage, the original word for praise is

tehillah—meaning "to sing a song or hymn of praise." More specifically, *tehillah* is a spontaneous, extemporaneous song outburst which is released from your heart. It's not scripted, rehearsed or found in lyrics which we could project on a wall or screen. Perhaps the song has never before been sung or copywritten. It is your personal expression of love to the Lord as you let go of everything bottled up within you.

Your song is unique, and no other person can sing it because it reflects the experiences you have birthed.

What I have just described is worship "in spirit and in truth." This combines the exuberance, the passion (or spirit), and the truth in knowing Who we are worshiping—Christ the King.

When we have these dynamics at work in our services, we fulfill what the Father is seeking.

THE TREE AND ITS BRANCHES

Look again at the analogy of Jesus and the fig tree in Mark 11. If God's Son went to the tree in search of figs, where do you think He would go to search for worship? I believe He would visit our churches.

You may ask, "Why not our homes?"

At this juncture, our spiritual culture has dictated that worship primarily occurs in the services which take place in the sanctuary. You see, we have not fully embraced the concept of worship as a daily lifestyle.

When Jesus first saw the fig tree, it was growing and had a healthy root system—it just wasn't bearing fruit. But because it did not possess what Jesus was looking for, He cursed it, making it wither and die.

I believe we can draw a comparison between the fig tree and our houses of worship.

The church represents the tree—of which He is the vine and we are the branches. The leaves are visible indicators the tree is alive, developing and growing. Likewise, it can be compared to the various ministries active in our churches today.

The "leaves" on our church tree include outreaches to children, shut-ins, prisoners, foreign missions and more. And we can't overlook Sunday School, the choir, day care, hospital visitation—you name it, we've got it covered!

MORE THAN FOLIAGE

To the average person, the church has appealing programs and all the signs of vibrant life. It is like the constantly changing foliage on a tree which is essential for our ecosystem. They provide shade in the summer heat, shelter in the time of storm and play a valuable role in photosynthesis—even offering a home to many of God's creatures such as birds, bugs and snakes.

So too, our church programs cater to man's needs and play a role in our social existence, but do they really zoom in on—and deliver—what God is looking for?

Jesus didn't want the leaves; He wanted figs. And although our programs may be beneficial, we have a problem if they are not what our Heavenly Father is seeking.

God is not impressed with institutions and agendas. He is in search of only one thing: our genuine adoration and worship of Him.

SHRINKING CHURCHES

Here's a truth we can't avoid. If Jesus cursed the fig tree and commanded that no one will ever eat of its sweet, succulent fruit again—and if that tree shriveled up and died—then what do we think will happen to our churches operating with dead programs?

Outwardly, our leaves and branches appear strong and healthy. We have large congregations and our coffers are full. We are not hurting for anything, yet we lack what God is seeking.

Could it be possible the Lord will declare a word over these churches just as He spoke over the fig tree? Will He say, "Okay, let no one else receive what he or she needs because the church has failed to teach or allow the people to give Me what I am hungry for."

Is this why we're seeing so many churches with shrinking congregations and their very taproot system wasting away? And, conversely, could this be why the churches who have intentionally given worship a priority and a focus as one of their core values are thriving and producing abundant fruit in the Kingdom?

WORSHIP IS A VERB

What is this "worship in spirit and truth" the Father is seeking? What does it look like?

I believe worship is a verb—it involves action and must be alive!

Worship springs from a relationship with the Father through the new birth experience. The "truth" portion gives us the biblical balance and the spiritual parameters in which we operate and express this worship.

The church has long been praying for the hand of the

Almighty to move, the river of God to flow and revival to break out in our land. Yet, in the vision the Lord gave me of the Throne Room, the currents of the river were only released through our worship.

Our *tehillah,* that innermost expression of adoration to the Father, is the key which unlocks the windows of heaven—then praise follows.

At this very moment, the Lord is seeking those who will worship Him in spirit and in truth. It is our praise, our *tehillah,* which ushers in a new dimension of the powerful presence of God.

CHAPTER FIVE

UNLOCKING PRISON DOORS

God is longing to hear the sound of His children's praise. But for many, it has been trapped and held captive behind a prison door. What once flowed freely as a river is now held back like a dam, restricting the waters.

The Lord is sending His Spirit and releasing His Word. With the Key of David, He is beginning to unlock those prison doors and is letting praise begin to flow. What has been confined within you is about to spring forth like a mighty rushing river once again.

In both the Old and New Testaments we read of the Key of David. The prophet Isaiah declared, *"The key of the house of David I will lay on his shoulder; so he shall open, and no one shall shut"* (Isaiah 22:22). And John, in his revelation, spoke of Jesus, *"He who has the key of*

David" (Revelation 3:7)—who declares, *"I have set before you an open door, and no one can shut it"* (v.8).

NEGATIVE VOICES

How does our praise become trapped and isolated? A major reason is because of fear and the opinions and rejection of man.

In an earlier chapter, I mentioned how during the beginning of my music ministry, a few people accused me of wanting to steal the limelight. As a result, when I was getting ready to sing, I would often hear their accusations ringing in my ears—and would hesitate, backing off rather than trying to expand my vocal abilities.

Yes, I sang, but there was a feeling of insecurity the devil held over my head.

I remember one service in particular where I was trying to lead the people in a worship song. Then, just as the presence of the Lord was about to descend, I heard those negative voices and literally shut down the flow of the Spirit.

Perhaps you—or someone you know—has been lost

in praise with the congregation when you sensed a feeling others were watching your every move. I even heard of one case where a member was blatant enough to comment, "Oh dear, singing isn't your gift. You can't carry a tune in a bucket!"

Such criticism stings.

What's holding you back from entering into God's fullness may not even be an opinion of man. The cause could be a sin in your past which the enemy continually taunts and reminds you of. Consequently, you feel unworthy and incapable of entering the Throne Room of His presence. As a result, you determine in your mind to stay in the outer courts of praise because the holy place is reserved only for special, sanctified saints.

This is a lie perpetuated by Satan himself.

YOUR SOURCE OF STRENGTH

God has a place, a time and a season for you to approach His throne because this is where His presence and purpose is discovered—and where His destiny and provision is released.

In His midst is where deliverance takes place, healings are manifested, blinded eyes are opened, deaf ears unstopped and those who are spiritually lame begin to find strength. It is also where those who have grown weary from the journey discover new life, *"...renew their strength* [and]...*mount up with wings like eagles"* (Isaiah 40:31)

Why do we shy away? What keeps our praise silenced? Why does Satan send his reinforcements to make sure the gates remain closed?

A Void in Heaven

In studying God's Word, the angel who was closest to the Lord was Lucifer. Scripture tells us out of him "piped" sounds and melodies (Ezekiel 28:13). He was the worship leader of heaven, yet the day dawned when pride consumed him and he tried to form a rebellion with at least a third of the other angelic hosts he had influenced (Revelation 12:4). His efforts failed and God literally kicked Lucifer and his entourage out of heaven (v.9).

I believe this left such a void in God's Kingdom that from this moment forward, the Lord began to seek, *"...those who worship Him...in spirit and truth"* (John 4:24).

The missing element in heaven can be found here on earth.

It is the *tehillah* we mentioned earlier—our

spontaneous release of praise and worship to the Father. This expression from our heart is what God longs for and what the devil tries his best to stifle. In fact, Satan attempts everything in his power to turn the tables and make himself the recipient of your praise instead of the Lord.

This is the reason the Evil One has you trapped behind a prison door and has kept your voice mute.

I have great news for you. According to the Word, the devil's door is powerless.

I pray as you continue to read this book and seek God's face, you will discover the key of David in your own life.

SILENCED BY FEAR

If there have been walls of fear, rejection, past sins, hurts or wounds which have suppressed your praise, it is only for a season.

The book of Luke records how the angel of the Lord appeared to a high priest named Zacharias, who was fearful at the sight of this heavenly being.

In the temple, the angel said to him, *"Do not be afraid, Zacharias, for your prayer is heard; and your wife Elizabeth will bear you a son, and you shall call his name John. And you will have joy and gladness, and many will rejoice at his birth. For he will be great in the sight of the Lord, and shall drink neither wine nor strong drink. He will also be filled with the Holy Spirit, even from his mother's womb. And he will turn many of the children of Israel to the Lord their God. He will also go before Him in the spirit and power of Elijah, 'to turn the hearts of the fathers to the children,' and the disobedient to the wisdom of the just, to make ready a people prepared for the Lord"* (Luke 1:13-17).

Zacharias, doubting, replied to the angel, *"How shall I know this? For I am an old man, and my wife is well advanced in years"* (v.18).

The angel answered, *"I am Gabriel, who stands in the presence of God, and was sent to speak to you and bring you these glad tidings"* (v.19).

However, because Zacharias spoke with a spirit of fear, doubt and unbelief, he was told, *"But behold, you will be muted and not able to speak"* (v.20).

When? *"...until the day these things take place"* (v.20).

Why? *"...because you did not believe my words which will be fulfilled in their own time"* (v.20).

Scripture records how the people waited for Zacharias and marveled that he lingered so long in the temple. But when he came out, *"...he could not speak to them; and they perceived that he had seen a vision in the temple, for he beckoned to them and remained speechless"* (v.22).

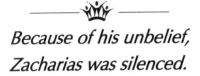

Because of his unbelief, Zacharias was silenced.

He did not receive the Word of the Lord and declare, "So be it unto me." Instead, he walked in fear.

Even though he was a high priest, Zacharias was seemingly under a curse because he and his wife Elizabeth were advanced in years and still without a child (v.7).

Here was a man who loved the Lord and had been faithful in service to God's house, yet when he had a divine encounter, anxiety and doubt brought silence.

THE BABY'S NAME

Keep reading this same chapter of Luke and you'll find Gabriel seeking out another person—a virgin named Mary.

He delivered a similar message; that she was going to conceive of the Holy Spirit. Unlike Zacharias, instead of rejecting the word of the angel, Mary's response was positive: *"Behold the maidservant of the Lord! Let it be to me according to your word"* (v.38). Then the angel departed.

Immediately, Mary rushed to the house of Zacharias to speak to his wife—who was her cousin. As they were talking, the baby inside Elisabeth, *"...leapt in her womb"* (v.41).

When her time for delivery arrived, Elisabeth brought forth a son. Scripture tells us, *"When her neighbors and relatives heard how the Lord had shown great mercy to her, they rejoiced with her. So it was, on the eighth day, that they came to circumcise the child; and they would have called him by the name of his father, Zacharias"* (vv.58-59).

The family became involved, suggesting other names. Then Elizabeth spoke up, *"No, he shall be called John"* (v.60). But they said to her, *"There is no one among your relatives who is called by this name"* (v.61).

So they made signs to still-silent Zacharias, wanting to know his opinion, *"And he asked for a writing tablet, and wrote, saying, 'His name is John'"* (v.63).

"HIS MOUTH WAS OPENED"

Why would he call his son by this name? Because "John" is the name the angel foretold in verse 13.

Finally, his physical man came into agreement with the spiritual Word of the Lord. This unlocked the door for a miracle.

In an instant, *"...his mouth was opened and his tongue loosed, and he spoke, praising God"* (v.64).

Zacharias' mute state was only for a season, but he learned much in the process.

I believe he thought again and again, "Oh, I wish I hadn't questioned or doubted. If only I had answered, 'As your servant lives, let it be unto me according to Your Word.'"

He was a high priest who was responsible not only for going before the holy place of the Lord, but charged with carrying out the letter of the law.

When Mary came to his home and announced, "I've had a visitation from the Lord. Gabriel spoke to me that I am going to have a baby and His name will be great among the nations, and He will redeem His people," I wonder what Zacharias thought?

GOD'S TIMELINE

Since Mary was not married, and it was his responsibility to carry out the law, this priest could have pronounced judgment and had her stoned. Yet, because he didn't believe Gabriel, the same messenger who now spoke to Mary, the thought likely didn't cross his mind.

This entire episode is not about Zacharias, rather his seed—which through John the Baptist had a prophetic purpose in the timeline of heaven.

You see, if John had been born when Zacharias was 19 or 20 years old, it would have placed him far ahead in the chronological order.

Yet God in His sovereignty knew exactly when Jesus was to enter the scene and how long it would take for John to grow up—and at what age he would be able to begin to gain a following, to develop a platform where He could declare, *"I indeed baptize you with water; but One mightier than I is coming, whose sandal strap I am not worthy to loose. He will baptize you with the Holy Spirit and fire"* (Luke 3:16).

The Lord was well aware of how many followers it would take before John could have an impact on them when he said, "Look to Him for He is the One we have been waiting for."

THE CHOICE IS YOURS

Like Zacharias, you may have been held captive too

long. Yet in your silent season, you have heard many things.

How will you respond when people criticize your approach to the Lord? Are you going to be embarrassed and back down when they say, "No, you can't worship that way"?

Also like Zacharias, your physical body must move into agreement with your spiritual man. When this happens, your season of silence will be over and you will find the release of the *tehillah* which has been trapped inside. You will be free and walking in the power of His might. Hallelujah!

The choice is yours. Are you going to call for a tablet and write, "Well, I guess you are right. I can't sing. I am unworthy to enter into the holy place"?

I say No! Rather, choose to walk in agreement with the Word of the Lord for your life and watch that prison door fling open!

Thankfully, God invites us, "Come unto Me. Enter My gates with thanksgiving and My courts with praise!"

WHAT IS YOUR ANSWER?

The world has no problem giving their *tehillah* to

Satan and his perversion through movies, music and the media. They even praise Madonna when she mocks the crucifixion.

Friend, there is One far greater than Lucifer. His name is Jehovah God and He yearns to hear your praise.

What will your decision be? Will you remain a prisoner, or are you ready to boldly declare, "Lord, I cannot contain my praise any longer. Even though it may be off key and I have made mistakes, I come before Your throne with brokenness of heart. I prostrate myself and offer my song of worship and my prayer of praise. I choose to break open my alabaster box and release my oil of worship unto You."

Your praise and adoration is no longer to be held hostage.

How do I know? Because I have heard from the Throne Room and declare that today you can be set free from every stronghold and hindrance of the past.

RECEIVE THIS PRAYER

Will you let me offer a prayer for you right now? Find a place of quiet solitude. Even though we are not together in person, this book is our point of contact.

I am asking you to *yadah*—to lift your hands as an act of surrender and submission. Also *towdah*—extend your hands in adoration and acceptance of God.

Receive this prayer today.

Lord, in the name of Jehovah God, the God of Abraham, Isaac and Jacob, I come to you on behalf of my brother and my sister. They have been held captive and their praise has become a prisoner to the strong arm of Lucifer.

Father, in Jesus' Name, I take the Key of David, which You told me to use, and I insert it into that prison door and unlock it in Jesus' Name.

I call the prisoners of praise to come forth and I curse what has kept them silent. In Your Name I bind every fear, rejection and the opinion of man. I nail these things to the cross of Calvary. I loose them and I call forth tehillah, that spontaneous extemporaneous worship of the King Almighty. May it begin to flow now.

Father, everything that has been a spiritual dam and blockage, I call it cursed in Your Name. They cannot change yesterday. All they have control over is asking forgiveness for their sin, making sure it's under the Blood and walking free in Your power and might,

Lord, You said to the woman caught in the very act of adultery, "I don't condemn you, but go and sin no more." So too, Father, I pray this for my brother and sister whose past has been held over their mind and spirit. Lord, we don't condemn them for their mistakes, but we likewise say, "Go and sin no more."

We declare the liberating power of Your grace and Your mercy to flow in their life. In Your Name, in agreement with the Word through which You have instructed me, and with the key of David, I speak for the prison door to be opened and remain open, never to hold back their praise any longer. I decree their silence was for a season which now has ended. The winter is over and their springtime has come as they begin to walk in the fullness of who You have called them to be and who You have created them to become—as they declare with their lips and sow the seed of praise into the heavens.

We declare this in Jesus' Name. Thank You, Lord.

OPEN YOUR HEART

I challenge you now to release the praise and worship

God is waiting to hear. This moment, in your private place with no one around, begin to flow in the Spirit. Open up your heart and offer these words to the Father:

Lord, I worship You. I give You glory, honor and thanks for redeeming me from my past and for enlarging the territory of my future. I thank You for Your amazing grace, Your challenge and Your provision. Let me walk in the freedom of Your power and might this day. I give You all the praise and glory.

In Jesus' Name. Amen!

CHAPTER SIX

WORSHIPERS ARISE!

As I was flying home from a conference, I looked out across the sky and was able to see the brilliance of the sun and the tops of the clouds. The Lord spoke to my heart and told me that He is calling us, the church, to a higher place in His presence.

For too long, we have dwelt in the low ground, often hidden from God by the dark clouds which cover the earth. The Lord is calling the church to mount up and ride upon the wings of eagles. In this elevated place, His children will find beauty beyond compare—and have a continual view of the Son, way above the clouds of worry, disaster and trouble.

It is time that we, the body of Christ, rise up—to move higher and dwell in the midst of God's presence. Leave behind the allure of the world and focus upon God's Holy Son as you climb above the clouds and soar into His presence.

Your perspective will be changed—you will see things the way that God sees them. Rise up! Do not fear leaving behind the familiar as you chart a new course into the undiscovered. Set your eyes upon God's Son and pursue Him with great passion in the beauty of holiness.

The Lord is yearning for us to praise Him. How He longs for us to spend time with Him in worship. Why does man extol his own work and neglect to give Him the honor He deserves? Why do we often allow the opinions of others to quench our passion for Him?

He is God, the Sovereign, the Holy, the Righteous One. We tend to withhold the one thing that He is seeking after and desiring. Oh, that men everywhere would praise God and render the love held deep within their hearts.

SET FREE!

Lucifer has always been jealous of the Almighty's praise and covets it for himself, but God alone is God and beside Him there is none other. He will have His praise come forth from the earth even if the rocks must cry out with exaltation.

The sun is setting and the time is fast approaching. Now is the hour to unlock these doors. For too long the heavens have been saturated with the blasphemies and cursings of His Holy Name as Lucifer parades across the earth.

I tell you today, praise will be a weapon to combat the darkness for it will be an illuminating force. It is time for the people to wake up from their slumber and sleep. Even now, we prophetically call forth praise to ascend to His throne.

This precious message continues to echo in my mind and fans the flame within my heart to continue on this quest!

A HARVEST OF EVIL

During my travels, my eyes have been opened wide to the reality that some cities have become immoral cesspools of drugs, prostitution and blatant sin. They sank to this level because they are simply harvesting the evil seed which has been sown in these places.

Through His Word, God has made it known that there are certain fixed laws, including, *"...whatever a man sows, that he will also reap"* (Galatians 6:7). This applies to both saint and sinner, *"For he who sows to his flesh will of the flesh reap corruption, but he who sows to the Spirit will of the Spirit reap everlasting life"* (v.8).

"CHANGE THE SEED"

I pray you are beginning to sense the urgency for a worship revolution. The seeds of sin must be replaced with those of praise and adoration to God Almighty. We need to plant so generously and abundantly that the crop will choke out every weed of iniquity. Now is the moment to reclaim our cities for Christ.

When you read the statistics of ever-increasing crime across the land, rest assured there is a spirit of sin being instigated and controlled by Satan. My spirit plummets when I pull up to a stop light and hear lyrics of rap music blaring from the car beside me—ungodly words promoting sex, violence and perversion.

My friend, when these seeds of evil are being sown so liberally into the atmosphere of our cities, why should we be surprised to see a harvest of murder, rape and depravity?

If you ask a farmer, "How do you change the harvest?" he will tell you, "Change the seed."

It's a basic principle: those who sow corruption will reap corruption. Thank God, the opposite is also true. When you plant seeds of worship, godliness, righteousness and holiness, this is what you will harvest.

SEEDS OF PRAISE

It is vital that we change from our self-centeredness

and begin to sow the attributes of God and the splendor of His majesty into the atmosphere around us.

With all my heart, I believe if we increase the seeds of righteousness over our territory it will result in an unprecedented spiritual turnaround—and a harvest of holiness.

Every time we audibly pray or release our worship to the Lord, we plant one more seed of praise.

TREASURES IN HIS STOREHOUSE

How then do we bring people to the point where they understand how to sow praise and worship?

What we plant must not be for a personal harvest; remember we are sowing into His Kingdom.

This is why it is absolutely essential that the words we offer and the songs we sing are never centered on us, but are directed solely to Him.

In understanding the etiquette of earthly royalty, there is a protocol involved in approaching a king. The monarch may listen to your problems and woes, but would rather hear you speak of the splendor of his domain. He is pleased when you compliment his efforts and it makes him even prouder of his kingdom.

Also know that when you praise a king it obligates him to be what you say he is—and to produce what you have declared.

SPEAK BLESSINGS

Let's apply this to how we worship the one and only true and living God—our King of kings. Instead of approaching Him asking for favors, we must bring Him our gift of worship. Tell the Lord, "You own the cattle on a thousands hills and nothing exceeds Your storehouses. Your righteousness, glory and grandeur are beyond compare."

The byproduct of our adoration is the overflow He releases back to us.

Understanding that the expressions of our tongue and our words are truly seeds, hopefully, we will think before we speak. The Word tells us, *"Death and life are in the power of the tongue"* (Proverbs 18:21).

This is why we must choose to speak blessings instead of curses. As we lift up our worship to Him, we are literally changing the atmosphere in our homes, cities, even the nations of the world.

FEAR OR FAITH?

God needs you as part of an orchestra who will offer this symphony of praise. Worshipers must rise up everywhere. Yes, God chooses to work through His children, but there are certain actions we must take to create an environment which welcomes Him.

Do your words invite fear, or do they produce faith?

If you read the story of the children of Israel, the fire of God's presence could have shown up anywhere, but He chose for the blue flame to rest on the mercy seat of the Ark of the Covenant. It was surrounded by the Levites who prayed to the Lord continually, every day of the year.

Why is this so essential? In the tabernacle of Moses, the Ark was hidden behind the veil—and only the high priest could enter this sacred place. The people never had the chance to gaze upon its splendor—only the smoke which hovered above.

Later, David built a Tent for the Lord, but it had no walls and was open on all sides. There was neither an outer court, inner court or holy of holies. Yet the flame, the tangible, manifest presence of God, rested on the mercy seat because the Levites knew their responsibility of praise and worship. This caused such a heavenly atmosphere to envelop the Ark, God continued to rest there.

KNOWLEDGE OF HIS GLORY

David is a role model for our worship, teaching us so much through His intimate relationship with the Father.

Biblical scholars believe that while David sat before the Ark of the Covenant, he heard sounds which were not made by musical instruments of his day. This is why they believe He ordered his craftsmen to fashion instruments so the music he received from heaven could be heard on earth.

The Lord wants to speak the same way today and is raising up a new generation.

It is the time spoken of by the prophet Habakkuk, when *"...the earth shall be filled with the knowledge of the glory of the Lord, as the waters cover the sea"* (Habakkuk 2:14).

This verse does not speak only of the "knowledge" of God—our libraries are filled with such information. Instead it is the knowledge of the "glory" of the Lord which will descend.

THE SOUND OF HEAVEN

In our worship experience, I believe God is calling us to a place where we will transcend normal barriers and, like David, be able to hear the fresh sounds of heaven.

This is also what John heard in his revelation. It was *"...a voice from heaven, like the voice of many waters...and I heard the sound of harpists playing their harps. They sang as it were a new song before the throne"* (Revelation 14:2-3).

As Chuck Pierce writes in his book, *Worship Warriors,* "When we worship, we ascend. When we ascend, we gain revelation from God. Revelation causes us to know the will of God and break out of Satan's conformity."

What the Lord has for you originates in heaven, yet we are preoccupied with our personal situation on earth —repairing the lawn mower and paying the mortgage, etc.

As a result we live far below the level the Lord has made available for us and in the busyness of our daily routine we forget we have access to His Throne Room.

A TIME OF PREPARATION

The entrance to His dominion is via the gates of worship. Scripture gives us the pattern, yet we must prepare ourselves to meet the King. As author and evangelist Dick Reuben states, "When the pattern is right, the glory falls."

When you read the story of Esther in the Old Testament, perhaps you will be surprised to learn she spent twelve months in beauty treatments preparing herself to meet King Ahasuerus (Esther 2:12). Only then was she allowed an audience with him. She found favor and was chosen as queen—and eventually spared the lives of her people.

This pattern is also true in our relationship with Almighty God. Remember, preparation precedes His presence.

A New Environment

No one is placed on this earth by accident. God has a unique purpose for your life and specific plans for you to accomplish. One of His objectives is to change the atmosphere on earth through you.

This purpose is discovered by spending time in His presence. You must be actively involved in releasing your worship in order to create an environment in this world where God's glory resides.

If we do this in our personal lives, the entire church is affected.

This is what the body of Christ is missing—and why

we so desperately need this revolution.

The "corporate dynamic" of congregational worship should reflect what we are experiencing privately. When this occurs, hundred of believers will unite together with the intentional purpose of creating a place where the Spirit of God is manifest.

EXPERIENCE HIS GLORY

I am convinced we spin our wheels going through man-induced form and ritual that the Lord's presence rarely shows up! But you may ask, "If God is omnipresent, how can this be?"

Please realize there is a dramatic difference between His holy presence and the *fullness* of who He is. Believers also tend to confuse His presence with His glory.

God's presence is very subjective.
Two people can be in the same service
and one may have a divine encounter with
the Lord while the other doesn't
appear to receive anything.

The *glory* of God, however is very *objective*. In every instance in Scripture where the glory of the Lord descended, it was experienced by one of the five senses. Think of the children of Israel:

1. They *saw* the fire by night and the cloud by day (Exodus 13:21).
2. They *heard* God's voice (Deuteronomy 5:24).
3. They *felt* the earth quake (Exodus 19:18).
4.. They *smelled* the smoke as God descended on Mt. Sinai with fire (Exodus 19:18).
5. They *tasted* manna from heaven (Numbers 11:9).

At the dedication of Solomon's Temple, *"...the priests could not continue ministering because of the cloud; for the glory of the Lord filled the house of the Lord"* (1 Kings 8:10-11).

This was His manifest, tangible presence—and I believe God desires for this to become a regular occurrence in our worship today.

A RELEVANT MESSAGE

A passion for God's presence will be the catalyst that will spark this "worship revolution." It will cause people to develop a disdain for over-polished performances pleasing only to man and will propagate events which are propelled by a longing for His presence.

I believe there will be a noticeable shift in the music industry which will cause broadcast media, both television and radio, to rethink their production paradigms. This new music will have such an effect on supply and demand that the recording industry will be forced to reconsider the way they produce their artists. This new genre will be one marked by the manifest presence of God and no longer by the polished post-production presentations of man.

As this new style emerges, it will cause worshipers and worship leaders who have been hidden in the house to become revealed.

Those who have been hidden in the caves will be brought forth, for it is their praise which God is longing to hear released into the atmosphere.

BEWARE OF IMITATIONS

Prophetically, I believe that there will be a divine calling on this emerging generation of prophetic psalmists. But rather than an upheaval built around man and his programs, this revolution will orbit around the Throne of God.

The secular music industry will attempt to imitate this style—but it will only be a counterfeit. Remember, Satan, the leader of their band, once directed the orchestra of heaven.

As you begin to yield to the Spirit of God, stand in awe and wonder of His majesty being outpoured, knowing the Glory of the Lord shall truly cover the earth even as the waters cover the face of the deep.

There are those who are in a state of transition, and many more will soon be. They have been boxed in by the dictates of religion and have grown restless with the status quo. They are ready for change.

THE SECRET PLACE

God is looking for psalmists to be released into this new level of anointing—those who are willing to pay the price and fully yield to His voice.

The Lord is asking you to move from the outer courts of praise and into the secret place where He abides.

As you draw close to His throne, flames from His altar will leap upon you and you will be set ablaze. These are not embers of judgment or purification, but reflectors of His glory. This will bring about such a transformation in your ministry, it will be obvious to both those who know you as well as those who do not.

Regarding the rebuilding of the Tent of David, as referenced by Amos 9:11, I believe the emphasis will not be on the form of worship, rather that all men, both righteous and unrighteous, will behold His glory. They will see and know the "I am that I am" — for beside

Him, there is no other.

Don't be shaken by the winds of change which are imminent. Make prayerful preparations for an encounter with the King of Kings.

PACK YOUR BAGS!

God is searching the land for people who will build a safe harbor for Him, rather than a sanctuary filled with man's agenda and selfish pride. His desire is not for the church to follow the world, but to hear His voice of instruction in the midnight hour and say "Yes" to His call.

Stand ready and be still. Have your bags packed, willing to move upon His signal and command. As He instructed the children to prepare for the Passover and the exodus from Egypt, so He will lead you on this journey into His Throne Room.

You are at the beginning of a prophetic move of His Spirit, yet there is much preparation still to be done. The seeds you sow are part of the process of reaping the great harvest ahead.

So, worshipers arise and begin to release your

tehillah—your spontaneous praise to Him. A sound needs to be birthed on earth which will establish a place for the Lord, and your praise is the key.

WELCOME TO THE THRONE ROOM

As you soak in His presence, He will begin to give you specific strategies and plans for your life and ministry. Don't become so engrossed in yourself and your needs that you fail to prioritize what must be in place before coming to Him.

The Lord is asking you to be faithful in this process.

As the king welcomed Esther, God extends His scepter and welcomes you into His Throne Room. He is saying, "Come night to Me."

CHAPTER SEVEN

A NEW SOUND OF WORSHIP

God is preparing to pour out a new sound upon the earth. Although it is what the church has needed for many years, not everyone will recognize its arrival. Only those who are sensitive to the Spirit and have been training and tuning their spiritual ears will be ready to receive this gift from above.

Just as a hunter learns particular sounds so he can bag his prey, what I am are referring to will only be heard by those who are diligently seeking the Lord with all their heart, soul and mind.

This heaven-sent sound will transform the airwaves. It will change people's lives and you will see a noticeable shift in the cities and communities which are listening and responding to His call.

Our mission is to be faithful and allow the Lord to flow through us. He is hungry for His people to burn once more with a holy passion for Him.

Wherever believers are seeking His face, God will meet them—and they can bask in each other's presence. It will be where He can deposit into them His blueprint and the specific tasks which need to be completed.

ACCEPT THE ASSIGNMENT

We must awaken from our apathy and complacency, tuning our ears to listen for His call.

As we will discover, when we release the sounds He allows us to hear, He will transform them into exactly what He desires them to be.

Be blessed and know you are the vessel He chooses. And remember, you are not the author and composer of the sound because it flows from the Father above—and none other.

When you accept this assignment, the Lord will go before you, clearing the path. He will be your covering of protection and His hand will be upon you.

DON'T INVADE HIS TERRITORY

What a tragic mistake to selfishly believe we alone can set the tone and present the sound of heaven the Almighty wants to outpour.

Prophetically, with so many decrees that a change is on the horizon, there are some who want to be the first to create whatever will satisfy this hunger. This is nothing more than invading God's territory and capitalizing on His desires. Why? Because such people see this as a marketing technique rather than a Kingdom dynamic. Sadly, they conclude, "If we can be the first to capture this sound, we'll saturate the market and profit by selling the most CDs."

Relying in our own strength rather than God's is the model of man rather than the pattern of heaven—and on judgment day we will be held accountable.

FASTING FOR DELIVERANCE

To better understand the impact of a sound from heaven, read the story of God's people when they came up against a powerful enemy.

The armies of Moab, along with those from Ammon and Mount Seir, joined forces to make war on

Jehoshaphat, the King of Judah.

He received this ominous advance report: *"A great multitude is coming against you from beyond the sea, from Syria; and they are in Hazazon Tamar"* (2 Chronicles 20:2).

Jehoshaphat was shaken by this news.

After seeking God in prayer, he proclaimed a nationwide fast.

The people journeyed from all the cities of Judah to pray and intercede for deliverance. Power was realized when praise once again became unified.

Then the king stood before the assembled throng in front of the new court and declared, *"O Lord God of our fathers, are You not God in heaven, and do You not rule over all the kingdoms of the nations, and in Your hands is there not power and might, so that no one is able to withstand You? Are You not our God who drove out the inhabitants of this land before Your people Israel, and gave it to the decedents of Abraham Your friends forever? And they dwell in it, and have built You a sanctuary in it for Your name's sake, saying, 'If disaster comes upon us—sword, judgment, pestilence, or famine —we will stand before this temple and in Your presence (for Your name is in this temple) and cry out to You in our affliction, and You will hear and save'"* (vv.6-9).

Jehoshapaht continued, *"And now here are the people of Ammon, Moab, and Mount Seir—whom You would not let Israel invade when they came out from the land of Egypt, but they turned from them and did not destroy them—here they are, rewarding us by coming to throw us out of Your possession which You have given us to inherit. O God, will You not judge them? For we have not power against this great multitude that is coming against us; nor do we know what to do, but our eyes are upon You"* (vv.10-12).

"THE BATTLE IS NOT YOURS"

It was quite a scene with the entire nation of Judah gathered together—husbands with their wives and children.

At that moment, the Bible says, *"...the Spirit of the Lord came upon Jahaziel...a Levite of the sons of Asaph,* [the chief musician] *in the midst of the assembly"* (v.14).

Here is what God inspired Jahaziel to say: *"Listen, all you of Judah and you inhabitants of Jerusalem, and you, King Jehoshaphat! Thus says the Lord to you: 'Do not be afraid nor dismayed because of this great multitude, for the battle is not yours, but God's. Tomorrow go down against them. They will surely come up by the Ascent of*

89

Ziz, and you will find them at the end of the brook before the Wilderness of Jeruel. You will not need to fight in this battle. Position yourselves, stand still and see the salvation of the Lord, who is with you, O Judah and Jerusalem!' Do not fear or be dismayed; tomorrow go out against them, for the Lord is with you" (vv.15-17).

What a powerful word from above!

When Jehoshaphat heard this message from heaven, he bowed his head with his face to the ground. Scripture records, *"...and all Judah and the inhabitants of Jerusalem bowed before the Lord, worshiping the Lord. And the Levites of the children of the Kohathites and of the children of the Korahites stood up to praise the Lord, the God of Israel, with voice loud and high"* (vv.18-19).

THE BATTLE CHOIR

Early the next morning they rose up, ready to march into the Wilderness of Tekoa. But as they were leaving, Jehoshaphat stood and announced, *"Hear me, O Judah and you inhabitants of Jerusalem: Believe in the Lord your God, and you shall be established; believe His prophets, and you shall prosper"* (v.20).

After consulting with the people, Jehoshaphat appointed a choir for the Lord. They were to march before the troops and *"...sing to the Lord, and...praise the beauty of holiness"* (v.21). They sang, *"Praise the*

Lord, for His mercy endures forever" (v.21).

The minute they started shouting and praising, the Lord sent ambushes against the men of Ammon, Moab and Mount Seir as they were attacking Judah.

What was the outcome? The enemy was utterly defeated.

The resounding echos of praise so confused the Ammonites and Moabites, they mistakenly attacked the soldiers from Mount Sier and massacred them. Then, further bewildered, they turned on each other and every soldier was slaughtered! (vv.22-23).

When the armies of Judah reached a site where they could overlook the wilderness, all they saw were, *"...dead bodies, fallen on the earth. No one had escaped"*

Then, as Jehoshaphat and his people arrived to take away the plunder, they found *"...an abundance of valuables on the dead bodies, and precious jewelry, which they stripped off for themselves, more than they could carry away; and they were three days gathering the spoil because there was so much"* (vv.25-26).

A PROPHETIC TIMELINE

What God gave the people of Judah that day was a brand new sound! He had caused a transformational anointing of sound to come upon Jehosaphat and his people. He caused their celebration and praise to be changed into a sound of war which was heard in the camp of the enemy.

I love how Jeshoshaphat confronted the situation. He earnestly sought the Lord and reminded God of His promises, telling the Almighty, "These people are willing to go out and fight the enemy, but You said, 'No!'"

We need to remind ourselves that God has a prophetic timeline and we need to be sensitive enough to know His schedule.

In the season you are going through right now, perhaps you are anxious and want to act in haste. You hurriedly remark, "Here's my plan for today." But the Lord gently restrains you, saying, "Wait! There is something great and powerful I want to show you. Follow My directions."

Your ardent praise is the key to His miracle!

Since Jehoshaphat was faithful in obeying God's

instructions, he listened to the Spirit-led message of Jehaziel—who was in the family of Asaph, the chief musician.

SPIRITUAL WARRIORS

The Lord has called those in music ministry to be spiritual warriors—not just singers or players of instruments. This servant of the Most High was willing to fight—yet God had another plan.

You are more than a worship leader or a singer in the choir or the congregation. The Lord has called you to be a secret agent for the advancing of His Kingdom.

The strategy God unveiled through this Levite totally revolutionized the battle plan. Wars had never been fought this way before.

Amazed, the people must have scratched their heads, asking, "We're going to put singers and dancers on the front lines? How can this be?"

Nonetheless, Jehoshaphat knew the voice of the Lord and was faithful to obey what God was directing. Because of his obedience, the Lord caused their sound of praise to pierce the earth. It reverberated across the wilderness and into the enemy camps.

The people of Judah marched forward with boldness—and a mighty sound of praise. It was a celebration, not a dirge. After all, you can't dance to a song of mourning. I can see them shouting, singing, dancing and holding their banners high as they marched ahead of the armies of Judah.

The frontline turned into a festival! Even more exciting, God caused the sound of their celebration and praise to be miraculously transformed so the enemy camp heard a mighty, invading army. For this reason they turned on themselves and there was total annihilation

TAKE IT BACK!

God can't transform your song if you never release it! This is why it is so critical for praise and worship to always be on your lips. Remember, the Lord simply says, "As you release the sound you hear, I will cause it to become what it needs to be"—this is the transformational anointing of sound we discovered earlier in this chapter.

There is a reverse mirror image of things in the Spirit. God's people see truth and light, while the enemy sees deceit and darkness. These are direct opposites.

Satan will whisper, "Go ahead; use your own strength in battle," but God says, "I'm going to revolutionize the way you defeat the adversary—to show you I am the Lord of Hosts."

In church circles we often use the phrase, "I'm going

to take back what the enemy has stolen from me."

There is no more powerful illustration of this in Scripture than the picture of the armies of Judah carrying the spoils from the defeated foe. It took three days to cart the goods away! You didn't have to convince Jehoshaphat, *"...the wealth of the sinner is stored up for the righteous"* (Proverbs 13:22).

TOTAL TRIUMPH!

Friend, allow the Lord to devise your battle plan. Stand on His Word which declares, *"Not by might nor by power, but by My Spirit, says the Lord of hosts"* (Zechariah 4:6).

It's your obligation to praise and it is God's responsibility to wage the war. If you're faithful in presenting your worship to the Father, you have freed His hands to battle on your behalf.

The same Lord who miraculously changed a rod into a serpent and water into wine can transform your sound of praise into a force which vanquishes the enemy and brings total triumph.

Are you listening for His sound?

CHAPTER EIGHT

READY FOR THE REVOLUTION!

In my two decades involved in full time music ministry —including over seventeen years in local churches, I've seen about everything you can imagine:

- Evaluation forms (I call them scorecards) passed out by the ushers for people to rate each aspect of the service.
- Mutiny from choir members because they were not chosen for a solo.
- The wrath of parents whose son or daughter were not selected to star in the Christmas program.
- Complaints from senior saints because the drums were too loud or the speaker volume was too high.

I've also directed choirs who reached new levels in their performance—then watched as their human pride almost wrecked everything we were trying to accomplish for God.

On more than one occasion, when I arrived to head a church music program there were members of the choir who were not living for the Lord—and living an active lifestyle of sin. Yet some in the congregation turned a blind eye, not wanting to lose their talent.

I came to the conclusion that if we cater to the flesh and continue to do so, we will reap carnal results. What pleases our ears and offers a show to man must surely bring tears to the eyes of the Father.

A PROGRESSION OF PRAISE

During a time in our ministry when I had been gridlocked in the outer courts of praise, a dear saint of God named Ruth Ward Heflin (she's now gone on to be with the Lord) wrote a book titled "Glory." In it she said, "Praise until worship comes, worship until the glory comes, and when the glory comes, stay in it."

This made me realize there is a progression of praise which must take place in our meetings. We often miss this because we're so concerned over the "order" of the service or what people think.

I can't begin to count the times a pastor has commented to me, "Keith, we've had a number of people say they don't like that particular song, so I don't think we should sing it any more."

I've also served in churches where the members and the board determine exactly what time a service should conclude—and if it runs five minutes over schedule, look out! You will hear about it!

What's the result? Eventually, the sheep—the congregation—wind up leading the flock.

This is not God's order or model for His church. Yet, we follow this pattern because so many worship leaders don't take the time to find the leading of the Lord regarding where they are taking the people in worship.

If pleasing others is our major objective we have lost sight of the fact God dwells in the praises of His people.

The "Praise Zone"

The first step in this divine progression is what I like to call the "Praise Zone."

This is the realm where man dwells. By nature, praise is horizontal in its focus—expressing what the Lord has done for us. You hear it in the words of songs with lyrics such as, "He healed my body, touched my mind. He saved me just in time." Or, "When I think about the Lord, and how He saved me, how He raised me. I want to shout, Hallelujah!"

These songs build our faith, encourage us in the Lord and help us connect with one another.

However, there is a danger:

If we stay in this Praise Zone
too long, we run the risk of placing too
much emphasis on ourselves—which
can result in an earthly "sensuality."

HE "WORSHIPED HIM"

Even *demons* are in awe of God and actually praise Him.

Once, while Jesus was speaking on the shores of Galilee, a demon-possessed man ran out from among the tombs. He was so tormented, *"...no one could bind him, not even with chains"* (Mark 5:3).

Yet, *"When he saw Jesus from afar, he ran and worshiped Him. And he cried out with a loud voice and said, 'What have I to do with You, Jesus, Son of the Most*

High God? I implore You by God that You do not torment me" (vv.4-5).

Jesus asked, "What is your name?"

The man answered, *"My name is Legion; for we are many"* (v.8). The Lord rebuked the demons and they fled.

Anyone can learn *how* to praise, but it takes an intimate knowledge of God and a heart-felt connectivity to advance to the next step.

THE "WORSHIP ZONE"

In our spiritual progression, we must move from the "Praise Zone" to the "Worship Zone."

This is where we make the transition from the horizontal plane to the vertical. No longer are we singing songs *about* God, we begin to sing *to* God. "Lord, You are Holy, and I lift You up and I praise Your Holy Name."

It is in this dimension of worship where the presence of God is near—where we invoke His fullness. The Lord becomes clear as the illuminating power of His glory is revealed.

In worship, we begin to see ourselves as God sees us, and our iniquity is exposed.

People who are living in secret sin feel uncomfortable

in a church that knows how to enter into the Worship Zone. They would much rather sit in a service which stays in the outer courts of celebration and praise—where they are never challenged or confronted by the Holy Spirit. There, they can praise, yet continue to live without being changed by God's transforming power.

The psalmist writes, *"Deep calls unto deep"* (Psalm 42:7). The depth of our heart is crying out for an intimate encounter with God. And the Lord is calling to your innermost being, "Come near, O you sinner. Come into My presence. Feel the warmth of My love and My embrace."

MOVED BY THE SPIRIT

When a body of believers enters the Worship Zone, it should not be odd or unusual to have a spontaneous altar call in the middle of a service.

Unfortunately, many ministers of the Gospel think an invitation to come forward can only take place after a message is preached. If we are not ready to respond to His Spirit whenever He is present, then our services are nothing more than singing, a prayer, an offering, an exhortation and a benediction.

If we are truly engaged in worship, the presence of God will so permeate the sanctuary that people are moved by the Spirit—wherever this may lead.

I've been in charismatic churches where they *think* they are worshiping because the atmosphere is festive, filled with celebration and praise. To an observer, it is exciting. The people are clapping their hands, swaying from side to side, and some may even jump or dance!

However, the praise abruptly ends when the music stops. There is no time allowed or spiritual direction given which leads believers into the zone of worship where the Father is calling us—into the deep things of God.

To progress beyond the Praise Zone takes an investment of our spirit, soul and body—and there are few congregations willing to make this effort.

Thank God, the tide is turning. The remnant is being revived, changing the way worship takes place in our services.

THE "THRONE ZONE"

Once we understand the Worship Zone and enter into it on a consistent basis, we are ready for the ultimate step which takes us higher. It is one we have referred to in previous chapters, yet it has a distinct purpose in our spiritual experience. I am speaking of entering the "Throne Zone."

The steps which lead to this place parallel the Tabernacle of Moses:

- The outer court is where celebration, praise and rejoicing takes place.
- The inner court is where sacrifice is made—and where reflection and purification occurs.
- The Holy of Holies (where the Ark of the Covenant resides) is where we have a divine encounter with the Father and the very manifest presence and the glory of God is revealed.

This final, sacred place is the realm we refer to as the Throne Zone.

A HOLY HUSH!

It is here we begin to experience the very *kabad* of God—meaning the "heaviness" or "weightiness" of His presence.

I'm sure you have heard the expression, "Boy, it was so thick you could cut it with a knife!"

I think back to 1997 when we moved from the jubilant, festive time in our music ministry to one of intense, intimate worship. Instead of an auditorium filled with high-decibel noise, there were times when a holy hush would sweep across the sanctuary.

Let me tell you from personal experience, the deeper you are in God, the more of self you will shed. Then, when you stand transparent before the Lord, there is such an awesome presence and magnitude of His glory it is almost impossible to stand or speak. You will humbly and quietly fall before Him.

A COVERING

I will never forget one particular Sunday morning as we were making our advance in praise and tapped into the Throne Zone. The presence of God was so heavy, nearly every person in the sanctuary was prostrate before the Lord. I had never experienced anything quite like it.

Literally, I was trying to find a way to cover my head.

I looked around to the gentleman playing the guitar and asked, "Do you have a cloth or something I can put over my head?"

He handed me an oversized scarf that I used as a *tallit*—a Jewish prayer shawl.

I laid on the floor and placed it over me so I could

shut out every distraction. But I was also so consumed with the anointing of the Spirit, I felt I needed the covering and protection.

At that moment, nothing else mattered —just the Lord and me under the tallit. In this place, I came face to face with the King.

YOUR REASON FOR BEING

The Throne Zone is the dimension where passion is ignited and purpose is discovered—when God speaks into your very soul.

As you can imagine, Satan uses every distraction to prohibit your entrance to this hallowed zone. Why? Because he does not want you to learn the destiny God has for you. I am convinced the reason people jump from job to job and from ministry to ministry is because they have never been close enough to the Lord to learn their reason for being—the objective they are to accomplish on this earth.

This is also what causes "burnout" in our lives. It is only when we know our destiny that we can love our mission and enjoy the task.

"BE STILL, AND KNOW"

Some congregations are so used to exuberant praise and worship, they don't know how to react when a true wave of God's abiding presence washes over the people and they stand subdued before Him.

Oh, how I pray that pastors and worship leaders will prepare believers to receive and respond to what the Lord desires—and teach the necessity of basking in the anointing of the Spirit, even if it means total silence.

A few pastors are afraid of allowing this to happen because they worry it could appear to border on some New Age expression.

Ministers would never need to fear if they would only take the time to share from the Word how God expects His people to worship Him—whether with vibrant praise or silent voices. Scripture tells us:

- *"Be still, and know that I am God"* (Psalm 46:10).
- *"My soul, wait silently for God alone, for my expectation is from Him"* (Psalm 62:4).
- *"Be silent, all flesh, before the Lord"* (Zechariah 2:13).

SEARCHING FOR CONNECTIVITY

A recent Barna Research study of the unchurched found they are not as interested in church programs or performance as they are in experiencing what is spiritual. They are searching for *connectivity*—and want to know if there is a higher power beyond their own selves.

In the natural, we try to use our logic and analyze everything that happens in a service, but you can't explain the anointing of the Spirit, God's presence or the power of His love—you can only experience it. And this is what the soul of man hungers for.

When I fell in love with Michele, I cannot give you an intellectual explanation of how it happened. All I know is the feeling was beyond words and the magnitude of my love for her continues to grow.

Equally important, she reciprocated this love, which made it intensify even more.

THE TWO PARADIGMS

The reason I call this third dimension the Throne Zone is because it moves you from a "democracy" paradigm to a Kingdom paradigm—where the Lord reigns.

If the King is pleased with your worship, He will extend His royal scepter toward you, giving the signal He is ready for a personal audience with you. In this place, He reminds you that you are His child and an heir to all He possesses.

Because you have invested your soul, spirit, time, talent and treasure into seeking the King, He welcomes you with open arms.

DEMOCRACY VS. KINGDOM

In America, we have a democracy model in government which is basically established by the vote of the people, yet we don't seem to understand a Kingdom concept—which is simply a decree issued by the King and responded to by the citizens.

If we are not careful, we will miss the entire Kingdom dimension because we are so concerned with the approval, fear or criticism of man.

Let's take a closer look at the two concepts.

The Democracy Paradigm:
- Focus is on self—"What's in it for me?"
- Performance driven.
- Patterned after our experience on earth.
- Produces the applause of man.

The Kingdom Paradigm:

- Focus is on the throne—"What's in it for the King?"
- Passion driven.
- Patterned after the worship of heaven.
- Produces favor with God.

When you are passionate, you are loyal to the King—and pledge your allegiance only to Him.

AN UNSHAKABLE SCHEDULE?

It is not unusual to find ministers of music who have a song list which is scripted three months in advance. They arrange the exact verses they will sing, how many times they will repeat the chorus and where they will make a key change. Then they rehearse and rehearse until everything is perfect.

This is totally opposite from the Kingdom order. Yes I believe in preparation, but it should be a schedule to depart *from* rather than an agenda to stick *to*.

Your objective should be passionate praise and worship of the King—and if He receives your first song and begins to usher you into the Throne Zone, you should be ready to toss away the rest of your list. You see, our focus is not on the slick production we have rehearsed, rather it is on whether the King finds favor with what we have offered.

The revolution we are discussing (1) changes the way we *view* worship and (2) transforms the way we *do* worship. I like what James says. "Faith without works is dead."

We can have head knowledge of what is pleasing to the Lord, but our hearts can be miles from the truth.

A theoretical understanding is of no avail unless application follows the theory.

More than an "Ice Breaker"

As on any journey, it's imperative we know where we are headed. You don't click onto MapQuest, type in your home address and ask for directions without giving a specific destination. Otherwise, you'll be driving around in circles.

In your spiritual walk, without a God-given purpose you will wander aimlessly through life. This is why you need to ask the Lord to give you a clear picture of your reason for being. He will not only show the objective, but give you check points along the way to let you know you are making progress.

Many worship leaders and pastors fail to see the big picture. They view praise and worship as simply preliminary music to precede the preached Word—using it as an "ice breaker" to gear up the congregation for the message.

Even in a church where the music may be loud and celebratory, the purpose of worship time is often missed. Let me remind you again—the message by the pastor is for *us*, but worship is for *Him.*

THE SPIRITUAL CLIMATE

Personally, I've come to the conclusion that God is more interested in our worship than He is in the exhortation from the pastor. He longs to hear our praise.

I'm certain there are those who will take exception to this, but there needs to be a balance in our services between coming into the presence of the Lord and listening to a sermon. To me, the present ratio of time allotted is tilted far more toward man than God.

It is our worship which determines the overall spiritual temperature and climate of a service.

A NEW ZEAL

I am encouraged by the number of individuals

attending our conferences. The Lord is stirring the hearts of these precious people, and they are returning to their congregations with a passion and zeal for the presence of God more than the approval of man.

There will always be criticism of the way some pastors or evangelists conduct their services. Yet I have been in meetings of these servants of God where you cannot deny there is an atmosphere of the anointing and God's Spirit is present. Millions have watched the telecasts where this power is present and hunger for the same Spirit to be evident in their own churches.

Read God's Word and you'll find that when the King of kings shows up, miracles happen. Individuals are healed and delivered, demons are loosed and people are set free. There is great victory.

In the Gospels, if anything was lacking—such as wine at the wedding in Cana—provision came because Jesus was there.

We will see a far greater spiritual dynamic occur in our services when we take the time to create an atmosphere in which the presence of God can dwell. When He is there, all things are possible.

THE NEXT DIMENSION

We're on our way to God's throne—not to a Broadway production with guest celebrities.

When a wise leader recognizes this progression, he will take the people from where they are to the place God is calling them to be.

Is your church headed in the right direction, or are you stuck in the outer courts week after week, month after month, even year after year?

When it's time for worship, do you sense the presence of the Lord drawing near, but are not sure how to reach the next dimension? Friend, it is there, just in front of you—waiting for you to forget the order of the service or the clock on the wall. Don't worry over the opinions of others, keep worshiping the Lord until there is a breakthrough. Just one person entering the Throne Zone, may be all it takes for His Spirit to saturate the entire congregation.

THREE KEYS

Where are you on this path? I want to give you three keys which I pray will help you discover the Throne Zone—and allow you to visit there often.

Key #1: Experience

The first level on which people connect is experiential. It is where we have a lasting impression of what we feel.

Think back to the day you gave your heart to the Lord and made a commitment to Him. Do you remember how you felt? Do you recall the atmosphere which was so pregnant with the power of God that the Holy Spirit caused conviction to invade your life?

*Can you remember how clean
and pure you felt as the blood of Christ
washed away your sin?*

Once you've experienced the touch of the Lord, you will never be the same.

WHAT KIND OF GRAVY?

In some of the sessions I teach at conferences, I have used an illustration that includes chocolate gravy. I don't know whether you've ever tasted this delicacy or not; I sure hadn't until I was visiting some of my wife's relatives in Tennessee a few years ago.

As I woke up, I could smell the aroma of biscuits

cooking in the kitchen, then I was told, "You're going to have some chocolate gravy this morning."

Immediately, I began to wonder how good or bad it was going to be! But since I like sweet things, I decided to give it a try. Being unfamiliar with the process, they told me, "Put a little butter on the biscuit and pour the chocolate gravy on top—just like any other kind of gravy."

This may sound gross, but when I took that first bite it was heavenly, and began to melt in my mouth—even better than a fresh, hot Krispy Kreme donut!

Even today, when I tell this story to those who have never tasted chocolate gravy, they think it's the oddest concoction they've ever heard of and doubt if they could ever eat the combination. (The recipe is on our website: www.hiscall.org.)

EXPERIENCE IT!

This is similar to people who have never personally enjoyed the Throne Zone, yet once they have a taste, nothing else satisfies.

When your priority is on heaven's realm, the outer courts of celebration will leave you hungry and wanting more. As Scripture tells us, *"Oh, taste and see that the Lord is good"* (Psalm 34:8).

Since taste is one of our senses, it's experiential.

To know what it means to be in God's presence, find a place of worship where this dimension is put into practice. Take advantage of entering into this atmosphere at events such as a Throne Zone Worship Conference, Kingdom Worship Summit or a Night of Worship —where people are encouraged to practice coming into the presence of God..

There is no substitute for personal experience, and this is the first level where people can connect.

Key #2: Education

If you begin the process by first trying to relate to people on a knowledge level, it won't work. Education and critical thinking is the second step, not the first.

Only after a personal experience are we ready to progress—remember, we shouldn't remain in the "feeling" dimension forever. Use the second key to unlock the door to God's Word. Study Scripture to know the "who, what, why, where, when and how" of praise and worship.

This "spiritual information" phase is critical. For me,

after witnessing some things of God I didn't quite understand, I dug into the Word and found the parameters and principles were already there.

WHAT DOES THE WORD SAY?

In my earlier days, I was playing the keyboard when the Spirit would move upon me, yet I really didn't understand what was taking place. Then I studied the Scriptures and read how the Hebrew word *"zamar"* defined what David did when he played the harp and calmed the spirit of King Saul. I saw in the Word this was an acceptable expression of worship I can release when I feel inspired by the Holy Spirit.

The same was true when I researched the term *"halal,"* and learned that exuberant praise is encouraged by the Lord. This gave me biblical support for my experience.

On my spiritual journey, when these dimensions of worship broke loose in our church, we took choir rehearsal time to give discipleship training on what God was doing. By delving into the Word and using other resources to help us understand the worship experience, it caused the depth of our ministry to reach levels we had never before known.

*We began to understand our role
as modern day Levites, and discovered our
purpose in the presence of Almighty God.*

Key # 3:Impartation

It is imperative for us to take what the Lord has revealed and plant the seed into the life of another person. This act of impartation is necessary so others will receive what we have experienced and learned.

For me, as I lay hands on an individual and transfer what the Lord has blessed me with, it releases what I hold and makes room for God to pour even more into my heart and soul.

I pray you will receive this key that seals this work in your life. Experience and education are necessary, but the worship revolution will not occur without impartation. It is the glue which binds it all together.

Will you climb these steps to enter the Throne Zone and release God's song from above? When you do, you will be fulfilling the words spoken by Jesus: "Thy Kingdom come, thy will be done, on earth as it is in heaven."

CHAPTER NINE

THE BIRTHING
PROCESS

The woman who pressed her way through the crowd, simply to touch the hem of Jesus' garment, realized a new dimension in her life. The moment she touched His robe she was healed from a sickness which had plagued her for many years.

It was her passionate pursuit of Jesus that caused her miracle to become manifested.

To the faithful and persistent worshipers who press their way through the realms of religious mediocrity and gain entrance to the Throne Zone, God promises He will be there, waiting to transform their lives, just as He did for this woman.

As we mentioned in the previous chapter, passion is ignited and purpose is discovered in the Throne Zone.

The *process* of purpose, however, is much like childbirth. It begins with a seed which is deposited—or imparted—into the spiritual womb.

There is a moment to conceive, then a time of gestation—when the baby grows within the comfort and safety of the womb. But ultimately, what you have been carrying within you is ready to be birthed into the world.

You may have become pregnant with purpose only recently. On the other hand, perhaps you feel as though you have been carrying your spiritual baby for 25 years or longer. Or, maybe you have completed the "transition" period and are now ready to give birth.

Let me illustrate by sharing this personal story.

"THIS IS IT!"

Michele and I were expecting our son Judah. When her nine months of waiting was complete, she turned to me one day and announced with urgency, "I think it's time to go to the hospital."

We had prepared for this moment and had everything packed, ready to go. After checking in on the maternity floor, the doctor examined my wife and said, "I'm sorry. This is false labor."

I'll never forget the look on Michele's face as she turned to me and exclaimed, "If this is what the pain feels like in *false* labor, we're in big trouble!"

We drove home and tried to get some rest, but the pains didn't stop. Two hours later we decided to rush back to the hospital. On the way, she kept repeating, "This is it! This is it!"

She was right! It turned out she had been in labor the whole time, so they performed an epidural to relieve the pain. Unfortunately, this process was unsuccessful because Michele had undergone back surgery several years prior and evidently scar tissue had formed which prevented the epidural from working properly.

A TWO PART CYCLE

Twenty-eight hours later, with no medication, she was in tremendous agony and pleading, "I want this over!"

We both were tired, frustrated, and drained emotionally and physically. Now it was me who was asking for pain medication!

Finally, friends who were waiting with us for the big event convinced me to walk out of the room, get some fresh air and relax a bit.

As I was closing the door, I saw a sign which read, "Labor and Delivery" and suddenly realized it's a two part cycle. Labor involves birthing pains but the delivery is when the child actually enters the world."

After a short break, I returned to the room with a cup of coffee in my hand. Immediately, my wife began complaining, "Where's that awful smell coming from?"

I couldn't believe her reaction. She *loves* coffee!

Unbeknown to me, Michele had entered into the part of the birthing process known as transition. In this phase, the body is actually undergoing a physical metamorphosis from labor to delivery.

For me and Michele, the coffee was simply an indicator we were in this state of transition. Perhaps there will be certain things you enjoyed in ministry or corporate worship meetings, yet now they leave you frustrated, feeling, "There must be more."

No longer do the ritual and motions of religion bring you fulfillment. Instead, you find they leave you with feelings quite the opposite—much like the coffee did for Michele. Transition simply means you are just on the verge of giving birth.

An "ER" Episode

A few minutes later the doctor was making his afternoon rounds to get an update. When he came into the room, the attending nurse said, "There's no change."

"Well, let me check her out," he replied.

As he began to examine Michele, he evidently used some kind of code language because immediately the quiet, relaxed atmosphere was transformed into a high-tension emergency room, similar to what you would see on an "ER" television episode.

Bright spotlights were beaming down from the ceiling, carts and equipment were rushed in and the room was totally changed into a delivery theater.

Seven minutes later, we were holding our healthy newborn son. We named him Judah Dominic—which means, "praise belonging unto the Lord."

YOUR TIME HAS COME

There is a direct correlation between physical and spiritual birth.

The Lord impressed upon me there is also a birthing time for our purpose—which has been shut up within our womb.

*We have gone through the gestation period
and the moment of delivery is near.*

How can we be so sure? Because it is a fixed law of God.

Perhaps you are in the midst of this process right now. You've paid the price of waiting and praying. Now you are investing your energy by pressing through and pushing into the Throne Zone—pregnant with your purpose and vision.

The time for the delivery of your purpose is at hand. It is your prophetic destiny.

DON'T RUSH IT!

When Michele and I were preparing for parenthood, we took Lamaze classes, and in those sessions I began to realize many of the same concepts for delivering a child apply to the birthing of our purpose

One of the first principles the instructor told us was, "At the beginning of labor, when you feel like pushing, don't. It's not time."

They informed us if you begin to push too soon, you could damage the baby, perhaps causing problems in the shaping of the head. And there is danger for the mother too, because there are certain parts of your body which must line up into the right position before you are ready to deliver.

*Spiritually, God's purpose for you
will spring to life at a specific moment
on His timeline. Don't rush it. When
you feel like pushing, relax!*

THE BREATH OF GOD

The second major point the Lamaze instructor shared was: "Breathe! As you take in oxygen, it flows into your bloodstream—and is piped into the baby as it makes the journey to the outside world."

This also applies to the spirit realm. Scripture tells us, *"God is a Spirit..."* (John 4:14). The Greek word for Spirit is *pneuma*—meaning "the breath of God."

Remember, at the creation of the first man, Adam, *"...God formed man of the dust of the ground, and breathed into his nostrils the breath of life; and man became a living being"* (Genesis 2:7).

As you enter this season of development, it is imperative to allow the breath of God to flow through your entire being, so what you have in your spiritual womb will receive enough divine oxygen from heaven to complete the journey through the birthing process.

If, for any reason, you restrict God's breath from flowing through you, it will inhibit the growth He has already begun. Should this happen, you will become weary and faint along the way.

DON'T LOSE YOUR FOCUS

Third, the Lamaze instructor emphasized we need to have a focal point. "Find a place in the room and concentrate."

Why is this important? When you completely center your attention on a specific object you develop tunnel vision and everything else around you becomes blurry. You may totally forget what is happening elsewhere because, like a magnifying glass, you have narrowed your attention and energy to that one spot.

This also occurs in the things of the Spirit.

As you are birthing your purpose, keep your eyes on Christ the King who reigns upon the throne forever and ever, and begin to praise.

By zeroing in on Him with all your mind, soul and spirit, you eliminate the confusion whirling around you.

I remember the friends who were with us in Michele's labor room. She was hooked up to equipment with a computer screen so we could see the oncoming contractions milliseconds before she actually felt them. "Oh, here comes a big one. You'd better brace yourself," they would tell her. Our friends meant well, but inside Michele was praying, "Don't tell me."

Anxiety and anticipation causes you to freeze up.

There comes a time in our spiritual walk when we need to dismiss the distractions of those who say, "You need to do this!" Or, "Do that!"

ADVICE FROM THE GREAT PHYSICIAN

When you are waiting in the birthing room, you only want the advice or opinion of the head doctor.

Likewise, as your destiny is about to be born, the one you need to listen to is the Great Physician, Jehovah God. By shutting out all other voices you will find the realm of peace which passes all understanding—the calm in the midst of the storm.

I believe the Father is preparing to birth His purpose in you. Perhaps at this very moment you feel the labor pains of your destiny. In God's perfect timing you will stand and declare His greatness and lead others to worship His Holy Name.

Will you respond to His call?

CHAPTER TEN

DIGGING THE WELLS OF WORSHIP

O ne afternoon, as I was watching a Christian television program, the host made this statement: "God has raised our ministry up for the purpose of building your faith."

His words grabbed my attention and, as I began to mull over them, the Lord expanded my vision. He showed me how each ministry has a specific assignment with the end result of providing Living Water to the body of Christ. I saw each ministry digging a well—so when people needed a particular nourishment, they could come and freely drink.

Immediately I thought of other major ministers, teachers and evangelists and it became clear:

- One has been raised up by the Lord to dig the wells of healing, so when people thirst for a miracle, there is a place for them to drink.
- Another has been called to dig the well of the Word, to provide refreshment from Scripture.
- Still others have been commissioned to dig the wells of evangelism, providing a place for sinners to drink from the waters of salvation.

These are all part of the Kingdom dynamic. He has raised up each of these "spiritual watering holes" for the sake of His work in heaven and on earth.

Never was it God's design or desire for each well to form its own doctrine or belief—which would bring confusion or division to the body of Christ. Instead of barriers such as denomination or race, His perfect plan is for the wells to be available to all: *"And whosoever will, let him take the water of life freely"* (Revelation 22:17 KJV).

WHAT'S THE AGENDA?

Then the Lord prodded my thinking by asking this question, "Where is the well for worshipers? Where can they go to find an oasis of refreshment and return to their churches with a zeal to bring people into My presence?"

The reason my wife and I pour our hearts into our conferences is to provide a safe place for people to both pursue and practice entering the Throne Room of God.

When I asked the Lord, "What should be the agenda for these events?" He answered, "There is none. Gather the people; let them sit and soak in My presence so that I can reveal the specifics and strategies for their lives."

Just as a simple sponge can absorb water and be taken to another location, God is calling us to "soak" and be saturated with Him—then to become carriers of His glory.

The Lord desires for us to literally squeeze and pour out waters from above over the lives of thirsting souls.

"Who Will Lift Me Up?"

Through the eyes of faith, I see centers of worship rising up across the nation and the world—where men and women gather to be touched by God's Spirit.

They will return to their churches with a heart to bring people into a new dimension in their spiritual walk.

Those who have grown weary in the battle, who perhaps have been bruised and wounded by the religious system, are also welcome.

"Who will lift Me up?" the Lord is asking, "Who will exalt My name among the heathen? Who will build a place for Me and make known My glory?"

INVITE THE FATHER

After the movie *Field of Dreams* made its debut several years ago, people have repeated the phrase, "If you build it, they will come"—and there are pastors who have used this line to justify expanding their church facilities.

The film centered around a baseball field built in the cornfields of Iowa. Later, while watching a DVD of the movie again, I realized how the world missed the major theme.

In the final scene, the father (who had passed away several years earlier) and his son, Ray, are playing catch—something Ray had dreamed of, but sadly, was never able to do. After this poignant encounter where the father appears, the camera begins to pull away and you see cars driving to that location from miles and miles around, as far as the eye can see.

Why were so many drawn? Was it because of the

novelty of a ball field in the middle of rows of corn? No.

The throngs were arriving because a miracle encounter was occurring—and they wanted to be part of what was happening. The son created what he saw in his dream for his father to return.

Instead of, "If you build it, they will come," the line actually reads, "If you build it, he will come." As believers we know that without the Father's presence, nothing else matters.

In the final analysis, our fabulous church programs and stunning architecture are not the answer.

Only when we build Him a resting place does He promise to descend and manifest His glory.

"CARRY OUT THE RUBBISH"

Many wells of worship have been dug, yet they are soon filled with dirt and debris.

For example, Hezekiah became King of Judah at the age of 35 and reigned in Jerusalem for 29 years. The Bible says, *"...he did what was right in the sight of the Lord, according to all that his father David had done"* (2 Chronicles 29:2).

In the first year of his reign he opened the doors of

the house of the Lord and repaired them. Then he brought in the priests and Levites and declared, *"Hear me, Levites! Now sanctify yourselves, sanctify the house of the Lord God of your fathers, and carry out the rubbish from the holy place. For our fathers have trespassed and done evil in the eyes of the Lord our God; they have forsaken Him, have turned their faces away from the dwelling place of the Lord, and turned their backs on Him"* (vv.5-6).

Hezekiah explained that by ignoring this house of worship, God had sent trouble and desolation.

Then the king made this statement, *"Now it is in my heart to make a covenant with the Lord God of Israel, that His fierce wrath may turn away from us. My sons, do not be negligent now; for the Lord hath chosen you to stand before Him, to serve Him, and that you should minister to Him and burn incense"* (v.10).

They had taken the house of God—this well of worship—and turned it into a virtual landfill!

Unfortunately, we see this desecration today with priests and pastors who are no longer sanctified. They've allowed sanctuaries to become social clubs and consequently, people have lost reverence for our God and King.

A Sixteen-Day Task

Hezekiah saw a turnaround. Scripture records how, *"...they gathered their brethren and sanctified themselves, and went according to the commandment of the king at the words of the Lord, to cleanse the house of the Lord. Then the priests went into the inner part of the house of the Lord to cleanse it, and brought out all the debris that they found in the temple of the Lord to the court of the house of the Lord. And the Levites took it out and carried it to the Brook Kidron. Now they began to sanctify on the first day of the first month, and on the eighth day of the month, they came to the vestibule of the Lord"* (vv.15-17).

Think of it! It took eight days of garbage removal just to reach the foyer area of the tabernacle—and sixteen days to finish the job (v.17).

Bring Out the Trumpets!

When the sanctuary was repaired and the altar rebuilt, it was time for jubilant praise and worship. Hezekiah, *"...stationed the Levites in the house of the Lord with cymbals, with stringed instruments, and with harps, according to the...commandment of the Lord by his prophets. The Levites stood with the instruments of*

David, and the priests with the trumpets. Then Hezekiah commanded them to offer the burnt offering on the altar. And when the burnt offering began, the song of the Lord also began with the trumpets and with the instruments of David king of Israel. So all the assembly worshiped, the singers sang, and the trumpeters sounded; all this continued until the burnt offering was finished. And when they had finished offering, the king and all who were present with him bowed and worshiped" (vv.23-30).

This was a revival!

The Bible tells us, *"...Hezekiah and all the people rejoiced that God had prepared the people, since the events took place so suddenly"* (v.36).

What the Lord is about to pour out from heaven will happen quickly—yet remember, your preparation precedes provision.

Are you ready to drink of the Living Waters? Will you dig the wells?

My Prayer for You

I do not know where you are in your progression of praise on your journey to the Throne Zone, but please allow me to pray these words with you:

Father, I thank You for my brother or sister who has taken the time to read what you have deposited in my spirit. With each piece of the puzzle, I pray the picture has become clearer.

Today, may the reader find strength and refreshment in Your holy presence and be ignited with a fresh passion for You.

May they be impregnated with purpose and discover destiny for their lives. Lord, no longer let them wander on a quest for self-worth, but fuel them with a fire from on high.

Stir up a holy flame and let their worship revolve around You and the throne of Your glory.

Lord, inspire them to build for You a resting place—a holy habitation—in their homes, their automobiles, their offices and in their churches.

I pray their praise will no longer be silenced behind prison doors. Let them walk in freedom. As they release sounds of praise as seeds into heaven, may the atmosphere change because of Your glory and power.

Father, as they offer their gift of worship, please bless them in return—physically, financially, emotional and spiritually.

Just as You sent Gabriel to Zacharias and Mary, may they have a divine visitation of Your angelic hosts,

God, I pray you will touch them this day and let a worship revolution begin.

Amen.

WORDS OF PRAISE

In the Hebrew language there are many expressive terms for praise. Let me suggest you incorporate these into your worship.

Barak—to kneel down, to bless God as an act of adoration. When used in Scripture it implies, "expecting to receive a blessing from the Lord" (Psalm 95:6).

Halal—a primary root word for praise—from which our word Hallelujah derives. It means to shine, to be clear, to show, to boast or rave, to celebrate, to be clamorously foolish. Literal translation: "to spin like a top" (Psalm 113:1).

Karar—to dance (2 Samuel 6:16).

Shabach—to address in a loud tone; to shout, to command, to triumph (Psalm 145:4).

Taqa (Taqua)—to clap your hands (Psalm 47:1).

Tehillah—to sing or to laud. A spontaneous, extemporaneous song. This is the kind of praise God dwells in (Psalm 33:1).

Towdah—this comes from the same root word as *yadah,* but literally means "an extension of the hands in avowal, adoration or acceptance" (Psalm 50:14).

Yadah—to throw out, to worship with an extended hand (Psalm 63:4).

Zamar—to touch the strings, as in instrumental worship (Psalm 1:13).

FOR A COMPLETE LIST OF CDs, DVDs AND
OTHER MINISTRY RESOURCES, TO SCHEDULE THE
AUTHOR FOR SPEAKING ENGAGEMENTS AND SPECIAL
EVENTS, OR TO LEARN MORE ABOUT HIS CALL
MINISTRIES OR THE "THRONE ZONE" WORSHIP
CONFERENCES AND "WORSHIP SUMMITS,"
CONTACT:

HIS CALL MINISTRIES
PO BOX 49307
CHARLOTTE, NC 28277

EMAIL: info@hiscall.org
Internet: www.hiscall.org